CW00537702

New Manager with Imposter Syndrome?

Imposter Syndrome?

15 Critical Leadership Skills for New Managers to Smash Self-Doubt, Overcome Anxiety, and Lead with Confidence, Respect, and Authority.

By Jesse Knight

"Success is not final, failure is not fatal:
It is the courage to continue that counts."

- Winston Churchill

Table of Contents

Introduction

I lean once again on the washbasin taps, staring at my reflection in the mirror whilst trying to calm my breathing. I splash my face with cold water and stare again.

My breathing is shallow, my thoughts chaotic.

The face staring back at me, reflects the darkest corner of my mind.
The imposter inside me. Clouds appear in my eyes as the mean girl in my head tells me of my failures, big and small, real, and imagined.

Voices in my head pull me in different directions, towards the light and back into the shadows…

"I am good enough; I can do this."
"You're such a fraud, you don't know what you're doing."
"What the hell is going on with you? Pull yourself together right now".

Thoughts and carefully selected memories of mishaps at my hand twist my insides so that fear takes another grip, my stomach tightens, and the tears come again. They pour down my cheeks uncontrollably.

This feeling is becoming all too familiar. More recently I've been able to give it a name: Imposter Syndrome. I recall a definition I once read;

"An attack of imposter syndrome is a period of intense self-doubt and insecurity. During this time, an individual may feel like a fraud or believe that their accomplishments are due to luck rather than their own skills and abilities. This can result in feelings of inadequacy and low self-esteem. Imposter syndrome can be a vicious cycle, with individuals feeling like they need to constantly prove themselves, only to experience more self-sabotage and insecurity."

I look back at the mirror, and in the reflection on the wall behind me, I see these words inscribed. Like someone before me has been here, feeling my pain, paying it forward to help me through this episode.

"Breathe, by Becky Hemsley."

I turn around and read the words, they speak into my soul in this darkest of moments –

She sat at the back and they said she was shy,
She led from the front and they hated her pride,
They asked her advice and then questioned her guidance,
They branded her loud, then were shocked by her silence,

When she shared no ambition they said it was sad,
So she told them her dreams and they said she was mad,
They told her they'd listen, then covered their ears,
And gave her a hug while they laughed at her fears,

And she listened to all of it thinking she should,
Be the girl they told her to be best as she could,
But one day she asked what was best for herself,
Instead of trying to please everyone else,

So she walked to the forest and stood with the trees,
She heard the wind whisper and dance with the leaves,
She spoke to the willow, the elm and the pine,
And she told them what she'd been told time after time,

She told them she felt she was never enough,
She was either too little or far far too much,
Too loud or too quiet, too fierce or too weak,

Too wise or too foolish, too bold or too meek,

Then she found a small clearing surrounded by firs,
And she stopped...and she heard what the trees said to her,
And she sat there for hours not wanting to leave,
For the forest said nothing, it just let her breathe.

I suddenly feel a wave of empathy and compassion wash over me, for myself and my situation. I am not alone.
There is at least one other person in this world who knows exactly how I feel. At least one person who knows what it's like to never feel good enough, no matter what you do or how much success you have. The loneliness of not being able to discuss it with others for fear of sounding like you are just attention-seeking or in desperate need of praise and reassurance. So much so that you spend your time alone in the forest or regularly sobbing in the office toilets.

My tears of frustration become tears of relief as my breathing slows down and my thoughts become more ordered.

Life will always have its ups and downs, like happiness and sadness, hope and despair, bravery and fear, but we all have choices. We can choose to remain optimistic; we can choose bravery instead of fear.

I remind myself that problems are not permanent. I am imperfect, make mistakes, and have emotions, but I also have choices. I choose not to be defeated by disappointment or fear.

Having conquered one moment of darkness, I look at the face in the mirror once more, the imposter slightly subsiding, and I repeat the now familiar mantra to myself...

"It will be alright in the end, and if it's not alright, it's not the end."

Imposter syndrome affects a significant number of people, but mainly women. Studies have shown that 70-80% of women experience it at some point in their lives.

If you suffer from imposter syndrome, taking on new leadership and management responsibilities can feel intimidating and challenging. Your self-doubt and loss of confidence can be incredibly debilitating and can limit your career advancement.

If you're already a leader or manager, you may well know the crippling fear that imposter syndrome adds to the role. This can be one of the biggest setbacks for achieving success in the workplace, but there's good news - you can take control of it, and you are most definitely not alone, in fact you are in very good company. Here are a few examples of other female leaders who have openly discussed their own struggles with imposter syndrome;

Sheryl Sandberg, the COO of Facebook and best-selling author of "Lean In," despite being one of the most successful and influential women in tech, still experiences moments of self-doubt and the fear of being exposed as a fraud.

Oprah Winfrey, one of the most influential and successful media moguls of our time, has publicly spoken about her battle with imposter syndrome. Despite her massive success, she has often felt like a fraud and that her accomplishments were not earned but rather a result of luck. Despite these insecurities, Oprah continued to push forward, using her platform to inspire and empower others, and through her work, she has shown that imposter syndrome is a common experience and that it can be overcome through self-reflection, hard work, and determination. Her story serves as a reminder that even the most successful people can still struggle with feelings of self-doubt.

Arianna Huffington, media entrepreneur and author, has also been open about her struggles with imposter syndrome throughout her career. She has said that she often felt like a fraud and questioned her own accomplishments despite her numerous successes. Huffington has credited meditation and focusing on self-care for helping her overcome her feelings of self-doubt and insecurity. Through her experiences, she has become an advocate for mental health and encourages others to take care of their well-being to tackle imposter syndrome and achieve their goals.

By learning how to recognize and overcome imposter syndrome, you can build confidence in yourself and your ability. In the short and long term, this can help you stay motivated and continue to climb the ladder of success.

I have a 30-year career full of diverse roles, challenges, pitfalls, and victories. Working in the predominantly male-dominated engineering industry, I faced numerous obstacles and attitudes that fuelled my drive to succeed.

In 2017, I left the corporate world behind to fulfil a lifelong dream of working in the African bush within the Safari industry, leading teams from different cultures, languages, colours, and backgrounds - something that imposter syndrome would have prevented me from doing in the past.

Writing this book is motivated by my personal journey of overcoming impostor syndrome and learning to keep it in check. I have written it to help up-and-coming leaders and managers find their footing with confidence by providing them with the tools they need to face their challenges head-on, no matter how daunting they may seem.

Although this book was written specifically for women stepping into new leadership positions, it has plenty to offer all genders and all leaders, new and experienced. It offers a solution to the self-doubt and insecurity that often comes with these roles. It will empower you to be able to lead confidently and without any self-doubt or sabotage.

I will share with you 15 crucial leadership skills, providing you with the tools you need to overcome imposter syndrome and build confidence in yourself.

With that said, it's time to delve into the first chapter, where we will be discussing the topic of leadership. We will explore the essence of what makes a leader and debunk the misconception that management and leadership are mutually exclusive. We will also redraw the lines of female leadership and reframe it in a new and empowering light.

Part I

Chapter 1 - In New Shoes

"I will not follow where the path may lead,
but I will go where there is no path, and I
will leave a trail"

- Muriel Strode,The Open Court

Defining the essence of leadership

What is Leadership?

Growing up in a small town, I encountered the reality of being a leader (or, instead, failing to be a leader) every year during my secondary education when "class prefects" were selected to lead the school's pupils, or "sports captains" were elected to lead the various teams, many of which I was a keen member of. Unfortunately, I was never chosen, in either of these cases, and the experience left me feeling like I lacked the inherent qualities of a leader and was meant to be a follower for the rest of my life.

However, with time and personal growth, I came to understand that leadership can be learned and developed. I studied the modern views on leadership and discovered that leadership involves inspiring and guiding others toward a shared goal. It requires more than just management skills; it encompasses qualities such as strong communication, empathy, adaptability, and a clear sense of purpose.

In this chapter, we will explore the concept of leadership, what it entails, and how you can become a leader, regardless of whether you were "born" with the necessary qualities or not.

How does leadership work?

Leadership is about having the skills and characteristics to inspire and motivate others. When you are a successful leader, you can effectively communicate your ideas, as well as the ideas of others, in a way that encourages people to take a specific, pre-determined action. When done successfully, you inspire people to act in a way that will bring about the results you want.

History is full of examples of people who had no prior experience in leading yet rose to the occasion in times of trouble and influenced others to take the course of action they directed. These people had specific characteristics that enabled them to assume leadership roles, and these characteristics, thankfully, can be developed and acquired. I remember those days in school, feeling discouraged after my failed attempts to be chosen as team captain, believing that I was doomed to be a follower. However, I refused to let my perceived limitations hold me back from pursuing a successful career as an inspirational leader.

What is the difference between leadership and management?

Though often used interchangeably, leadership and management are not the same thing. Both require you to manage resources; however, leadership encompasses additional qualities. Managers, for example, may or may not be viewed as inspiring, while leaders must motivate and encourage those they lead.

Leaders prioritize innovation over other considerations. A manager focuses on motivating her team to meet objectives within company parameters. At the same time, a leader is much more likely to set and aim for ambitious goals, even when it means disregarding pre-existing policies. When an employee presents a novel way of approaching a problem, for example, leaders will likely support them in pursuing it. While managers may be more likely to maintain the status quo due to their position within the structure, with superiors above them influencing their decisions. Leaders, however, tend to have more autonomy, allowing them to take on greater risks.

In my early career, I believed that a good team leader always maintains a peaceful work environment and that it was my job to create harmony in my teams. While this is an admirable goal, today, I realize that this is the role of a manager (to some extent at least) and that it is to be expected that true leadership will, from time to time, cause disruption and discord. This is par for the course simply because your job is to lead the business forward and innovate.

Innovation inevitably causes discomfort amongst team members as structures change, and uncertainty (the enemy of the comfort zone) reigns. While it can sometimes be difficult, this disruption is necessary to create a successful organization.

Leadership is much more than just executing tasks – it requires a combination of trust, action, perspective, focus, vision, and effective communication skills. These elements help build a strong foundation to motivate and inspire your team, driving positive results;

Trust means understanding and having empathy with your employees. As a leader, it is essential to define yourself by your intentions and actions towards others, building trust that your employees can see and feel. Heidi Grant Halvorson, professor at Columbia University and author of 99U, emphasizes that when team members trust their leader, commitment to and collaboration towards team goals are heightened, communication is improved, and creativity and productivity increase. To successfully achieve this, it is essential to understand how your employees think and what is important to them.

Action in leadership involves following through on commitments. Acting on what you say you will do. That doesn't mean the leader has to personally do it all. One strategy, introduced by Innovation Consultant Innosight, is to create a "Chief Bottleneck Buster." It reinforces trust in the team, showing that the leader believes in their ability to complete the task.

Perspective is crucial, it means ensuring that you take different viewpoints into account. You have your own outlook, which helps you set a goal and devise a plan to reach it. What is more difficult is incorporating other people's points of view. A way to define leadership is understanding what each of your team members is thinking and what drives them.

Focus involves dedication to implementing ideas and initiatives. A leader naturally motivates and involves everybody in whatever is happening. However, genuinely extraordinary leaders delve deeper and concentrate; an essential aspect of leadership is steering the realization of schemes and projects. As Peter Economy from Inc. Magazine, put it - leaders "set up policies, systems, and protocols in order that peak performance is concrete, clearly defined, and kept track of."

Vision is a key ingredient, and I cannot overstate the significance of having a vision. Although identifying a vision can be challenging, true vision is easily recognizable because it is inspiring. When people believe in a vision, they become motivated and committed to supporting it with enthusiasm.

Strong communication skills are essential for cultivating understanding, collaboration, and trust between team members. To be an effective leader, you need to be a strong communicator, as well as an excellent listener. Without communication, even the most defined leadership structure will not work.

Lessons in leadership

According to Simon Sinek, leadership involves inspiring and uniting a group through a shared vision while empowering them to work towards its realization. He considers leaders to be those who place the needs of their followers ahead of their own, with a strong sense of empathy and concern for the well-being of their team. To Sinek, successful leadership creates a supportive and uplifting environment where individuals feel secure, respected, and motivated to perform their best.

Trust and cooperation, according to Sinek, are necessary and not common in organizations. He says that every leader can have the qualities of empathy and perspective, which can help create successful organizations. Leadership is not about power or authority but about caring for those being led. Unfortunately, many highly skilled professionals are promoted to managerial roles without proper leadership training, leading to the creation of managers rather than leaders.

Leaders must shift their focus from just completing tasks to being accountable for the individuals responsible for them. Regarding the role of a CEO, he stresses that their responsibility lies not with the customer directly but with the people who manage the teams that serve the customers.

There are two approaches to exerting influence - manipulation, and inspiration. Manipulation relies on using incentives and consequences to govern behaviour, whereas inspiration creates a trustworthy and collaborative atmosphere where people are motivated to perform at their highest level.

The Litmus Test of Leadership is a straightforward yet significant evaluation tool for determining a leader's proficiency. It operates by inquiring from those who report to the leader about their feelings towards going to work daily. If the employees are content and enthusiastic about going to work, it indicates the leader's success in their position. Conversely, if the workers are disgruntled and have a negative attitude towards work, it suggests the leader is not fulfilling their leadership duties.

Sinek tells a story about a barista at the Four Seasons Hotel. The barista would ask each guest visiting the coffee bar about their day, take their order with a cheerful demeanour, and wish them a great day ahead. This small act of empathy made the guests feel valued and appreciated, often leading to generous tips for the barista. When asked why he appeared so happy at work, the barista replied that his managers always asked about his needs and were concerned about his well-being, making him feel fulfilled in his job. However, the same barista had a different experience at Caesars Palace, where he kept to himself and didn't interact much with customers due to the high levels of criticism and micromanagement he experienced there. This story illustrates that employees can have vastly different experiences and outputs based solely on how they are treated.

Prioritizing shareholders over employees' welfare and disregarding their well-being is thankfully a thing of the past, as it is detrimental to both the individual and the company. Leaders should strive to build a culture of trust, collaboration, and understanding where employees feel comfortable being transparent and asking for assistance.

We don't always have to be right or win to lead successfully. After empathy and understanding come perspective, and in business, it is about understanding the game you are playing. In game theory, there are two types of games: finite games, where the purpose is to win, and infinite games, where the aim is to keep the game going.

I remember the first time I attended leadership training having had no idea about these principles. We were each given a tray with resources to create a collage, some people having more than others. I was lucky enough to have a lot, and I thought of it as a finite game; I had to win. When others asked me to share, I refused - even though I had more than I needed for the task at hand. Observation revealed the more experienced leaders shared their resources freely, even to the point of having little left for themselves. They had chosen to empower the other team members to continue playing and ensured that everyone in the team felt like a necessary component.

These experiences taught me that leadership is not about winning or losing but about helping others and contributing to a larger, collective success.

Ten distinct viewpoints on the characteristics of effective leadership

We have seen that perspective is essential in leadership, so here are some powerful insights from the pens of leaders today on what it takes to be an effective leader:

"It's about having faith in your beliefs. You can't expect others to consider you a leader unless you have solid faith in your ideas..." (Matei Gavril, CEO at PrMediaOnline)

"Great leaders make the hard choice and self-sacrifice in order to enhance the lives of others around them..." (Joel Farar, Farar Law Group)

"Having the ability to show respect, empathy, and care to those that follow you, are all attributed to being a great leader..." (Brandon Swenson, SEO Pros)

"Knowing the strengths and weaknesses of every individual to effectively manage the outcome of a team is imperative for success..." (Alex Gerasimov, Insomnia Escape Room DC)

"A great leader understands that it is the people they lead that ultimately determines the success or failure of any venture..." (Randy Soderman, Founder of Soderman Marketing SEO)

"A great leader possesses a clear vision, is courageous, has integrity, honesty, humility, and clear focus..." (Bhagi Rath, Mattress Inquirer, Do Your Research to Find a Great Bed)

"Great leaders have clarity of purpose and are great at articulating their beliefs..." Amas Tenumah, CEO BetterXperience)

"Great leadership is determined by one's periodical blend of personal humility and unparalleled will to lead others in service of a cause bigger than themselves..." (Jake Rheude, Director of Business Development for Red Stag Fulfilment)

"Someone who leads by positive direction and builds agreement among its group members towards the accomplishment of a coordinated goal..." (Kara Kelly, Executive Director of CompleteContents.com)

"A great leader does not lead by forcing people to follow. Instead, a great leader motivates people..." (Mike Dan, SMS Marketing)

As a leader, you must maintain a dedicated focus, persist in your efforts, and assemble a disciplined, results-oriented team. Without a team, it is impossible to be an effective leader. By taking into consideration these ten distinct perspectives, you can gain valuable insight while also recognizing certain shared characteristics. To become a successful leader, you must continue your personal and professional development. You should likewise invite honest feedback from your team and take appropriate steps to improve on it.

What leadership is not

Leadership has nothing to do with your rank or place in the hierarchy of a company, and it is not linked to your title either. Many people mistakenly assume that the senior-most executives in the organization are the leadership. These people are merely senior-level executives. Just because one has a high salary, or a certain job title doesn't guarantee leadership ability.

Leadership is also not based on personal traits such as being outgoing or charismatic. This realization came later in my career. Looking back at my school years, I now understand that the selection criteria for youth leadership positions were likely based on popularity, driven by factors like extroversion and charisma, rather than the essential qualities required for effective leadership that we have discussed in this chapter.

Peter Drucker's statement, "The only definition of a leader is someone who has followers," is also outdated and incomplete. While a leader may have followers, true leadership is much more than simply having a large following. A leader should be a positive influence, inspiring and motivating their followers, in addition to having the ability to make difficult decisions and guide their team to success. A leader who is defined solely by the number of followers they have is more akin to a commander, lacking true leadership qualities.

You may also come across simplistic definitions of leadership like: "Leadership is the capacity to translate vision into reality." (Warren Bennis), "...leaders will be those who empower others." (Bill Gates), and "Leadership is influence - nothing more, nothing less." (John Maxwell). These definitions, although they sound decent, leave out essential components like a team, a vision, and overriding empathy, making them misleading and incomplete.

True leaders have an inner knowing of who they are and what they stand for, which is reflected through their commitment to their values and the principles they follow, regardless of the situation.

Redefining Female Leadership

Can you make for a better leader in a world dominated by men? Decades of research into leadership have revealed a clear answer: Yes, women can make better leaders than men.

An analysis of 99 sample leadership studies found that gender doesn't influence the effectiveness of leaders. However, studies also discovered that while male leaders rate themselves higher on leadership skills, supervisors and subordinates rated female leaders as more effective.

It's time to recognize that women can be just as effective, if not more effective, leaders than men. By leveraging the unique qualities that women bring to the table, like communication and conscientiousness, we can create an environment of powerful and successful, if not transformational, leadership.

Behaviours that suggest women are better leaders are their consistency in rewarding good behaviour and their avoidance of 'crisis management' (only intervening when things go wrong). Women also tend to be more democratic in their leadership style, as opposed to the autocratic style favoured by some male leaders. Women are accepted to be better listeners, communicators, and more inclusive decision-makers.
Female leaders spend more focus on building strong interpersonal relationships and creating an environment where team members can thrive as individuals and as employees. They are less focused on 'managerial' functions such as meeting standards and completing tasks but rather on building relationships and creating an environment where everyone can succeed.

Research shows that when women oversee household spending, access to education and healthcare for the family drastically improves. On a global scale, increased female representation in leadership has a measurable impact on economic equality, peace agreements, and the profitability of companies. In fact, when women are appropriately represented in the leadership of companies, there is a 21% increased chance of outperforming other companies in terms of profitability. Investing in female representation can ensure a brighter future for everyone.

Why, then, are there not more female leaders? Our downfall is often rooted in our tendency to underestimate our own capabilities, leading to a lack of confidence, and undervaluing ourselves in the business world. The causes of this are complex and varied, ranging from self-imposed limitations to cultural influences. By exploring these issues in more detail, we can better understand them and develop strategies to help us overcome these mental barriers.

The methods women employ to navigate gender-specific leadership norms

Female leaders are often put in the challenging position of needing to exhibit warm characteristics (which society usually expects from women), competence, and toughness (which society usually expects from men and leaders) simultaneously. This contradiction can create an inner struggle for female leaders, thus leading to a sense of "multiple personas" as we attempt to balance these seemingly opposite roles.

As a female leader, you may find yourself in several contradictory situations. You must show that you are both demanding and caring, authoritative and participative, advocating for yourself and serving others. You need to maintain a level of formality while still being approachable. Balancing these four paradoxes is crucial for you to lead effectively.

I've encountered all these paradoxes as a female leader throughout my career. One instance stands out in my memory. During a leadership training program, I was tasked with advocating for a point of view on a controversial topic. I was determined to win the argument, even though I disagreed with the point of view I was assigned, my powers of persuasion kicked into high gear, and I managed to convince the entire group to agree with me. However, after the exercise, I felt like I had intimidated the group into agreement and was regretful and embarrassed.

I opened up to the facilitator and shared my feelings with her. She told me that I couldn't have it both ways, that I had to choose between winning and pleasing the group. I struggled to understand this concept for a long time and spent many hours trying to find a solution.

In another scenario, I noticed that the group mistreated one of my teammates when he disagreed with a definition being debated. Determined to nurture an environment where diverse opinions are valued, I supported the team member and encouraged him to articulate his perspective. However, this resulted in me being mocked for being intellectually limited and not aligning with the "correct" viewpoint. It is sometimes challenging to find the right balance. Fortunately, there are strategies that you can use to reconcile these conflicting demands, which we will delve into in the upcoming chapters.

Why we need more female leaders

Conrad Liveris, an Australian economist, recently studied Australia's top 200 significant businesses using publicly available information. His findings were shocking. There are more CEOs named Andrew than there are female CEOs, indicating that more males in Australia have their first name in the higher levels of corporate governance than women.

This trend is not limited to Australia, as the United States also experiences a similar situation. Only 7.2% of Fortune 500 CEOs are women, occupying only 25% of top-level C-suite positions in the top 1000 corporations. The power imbalance in the business world is apparent and indicates the need for greater progress toward gender equality.

What could be the reason that this disparity still exists today? When we consider modern definitions of leadership and the traits that make a great leader, it becomes apparent that women *are* capable of fulfilling leadership roles.

Women have superior communication skills, which we can use to engage in more productive conversations with our superiors, colleagues, and partners. This leads to clear and open lines of communication, promoting a sense of clarity and understanding.

We bring fresh perspectives, innovation and varied perspectives which lead to better decision-making. We also lead more effectively, and many consider our female empathy to be our strongest superpower. We hone this ability throughout our life due to the various roles we take on. As empathetic leaders, we appreciate that people often interpret the world differently without being critical. We can connect with our team, engaging in open communication and understanding their challenges. Instead of imposing solutions or instructions, we listen to our team, helping them reach their full potential.

Women are skilled at handling crises, often bringing the compassion and patience honed from their experience as trained caregivers, particularly mothers. In times of emergency, these qualities are especially valuable for female leaders.

Data from the United Nations shows that globally, women earn 84 percent of what men do, resulting in a 16 percent pay gap. Despite decades of progress, this disparity persists in the workplace. One solution to this issue is promoting women into leadership roles within organizations.

Mentorship is another area where women leaders bring unique qualities. The impact of having a mentor, especially for younger individuals, cannot be overstated. Regardless of gender, everyone needs someone to guide them as they progress in their careers. With traits such as understanding, determination, strategy, and awareness, women excel as mentors and provide valuable assets to those we mentor.

Female leaders, especially new-time ones, often face overwhelming obstacles that hinder our growth and advancement in the corporate world. However, the good news is that leadership has evolved to encompass a wide range of characteristics and skills, many of which come naturally to women, and despite these valuable female contributions not always being recognized in the business world, positive changes are underway.

By continuing the conversation and empowering ourselves with knowledge and understanding, we can better navigate the obstacles we face.

In the upcoming chapter, we will explore the specific challenges that leaders encounter, providing insights that can help you prepare for and manage these obstacles. Knowing that these challenges are universal and that you are not alone can be empowering. By taking charge and creating your own outcomes, even in challenging times, you can achieve success as a leader.

Chapter 2 - A Steeper Climb

"Only those who will risk going too far can possibly find out how far one can go."

- T.S. Eliot,
Preface to Transit of Venus: Poems by Harry Crosby (1931)

Leadership is a vital ingredient in any organization that wants to make positive changes in the world, and guiding a team toward realizing a shared vision and communicating it with clarity is one of the most rewarding creative endeavours you will ever undertake. However, it is also one of the most challenging; for example, you may find that some people seem to be natural leaders, making you feel inadequate in comparison. Yet, with the right approach, anyone can learn to align teams towards a common goal and achieve remarkable outcomes, whether that be designing groundbreaking new technologies or simply completing a project on time and within budget.

The sad truth is that many of us fail to ever recognize our own leadership potential because when our abilities are first tested, we sometimes run away, scared never to try our hand at it again. It is true that leading a team is an arduous task that demands a combination of internal and external resources, requiring you to delicately balance the management of a diverse group of individuals, so becoming a good leader will take time and effort, but it will be worth it.

I had my first leadership experience when I was 22 years old and had just started working with a formidable female leader whom we shall call Sharon. She was the only female director in a male-dominated corporation, where gentleness had no place, and showing any signs of weakness could have cost her position. To earn the trust of her male colleagues, Sharon presented herself as a fierce warrior, exerting almost militant control over the teams she worked with.

Behind the scenes, however, she had built a trusting relationship with each of her team members. They achieved extraordinary things together, working in chaotic harmony, where, despite the hardness of the environment, they managed to create a safe place where they all could use their talents and abilities to build something greater than themselves.

After a few months of working with Sharon, I learned she had fallen pregnant unexpectedly. After 10 years of focusing almost exclusively on her work, she now had a new demand on her time and energy, and no one seemed to be prepared for the changes that would take place.

I fondly remember her team members protecting her and acting as gatekeepers to her office when she was too ill to work. Sometimes, she felt so unwell that she had to rest in her office, and the team would fill in for her where they could and cover for her where they needed to, refusing to let the outside world know that she may have been battling to cope.

As her due date approached, she left the office, and the team were left without their leader. As a trusted colleague and the only person with the necessary knowledge to step into Sharon's shoes, I was asked to take charge of a large project during her maternity leave. Stepping into the role of leading a team of people in a highly stressful and competitive world was a giant leap; I was considerably younger than most team members. They had spent years building the business alongside their leader.

When I was first offered the temporary leadership position, I assumed it would be straightforward; I had been doing the same work as Sharon, understood the technical aspects, and got along with the team.

It turned out that my four months of leadership would be a rocky road of trial and error. It was more challenging than she made it look! Today, I am grateful for the lessons I learned during that time.

Typical leadership challenges new leaders experience

Below are some of the challenges that I faced as a new leader. The latter half of this book will give you the tools you need to deal with them, but by understanding what they might be, anticipating them and then preparing for them, you will be better able to equip yourself to overcome them in your own leadership journey.

Providing inspiration and motivation to others

As a complete novice team leader, motivating and inspiring my team posed a huge challenge. I constantly questioned why they lacked enthusiasm, discipline, and motivation. However, I soon realized I was responsible for keeping the team aligned and focused on our objectives rather than blaming them for underperforming.

On reflection, I realized that some team members struggled to follow me because I was recently so much their junior, still the "newbie" learning from them. Many believed they could do a better job than me, and they may have been right at the time. My transition to a leadership position created unease in me and some team members, often making for an awkward situation.

Furthermore, I harboured a lot of fear regarding my role. Having only recently mastered my previous responsibilities, I was apprehensive about making mistakes. Aware of my inexperience, I felt insecure about how older team members perceived me. Rather than being the inspiring leader they had known for years, they were left with a new leader who feared them more than they respected her. This experience taught me that leading people toward a greater goal is impossible when you cannot see past the fog of your own fear and uncertainty.

Seeing team members as individuals

As a new leader, it's easy to confuse management with leadership and view employees as machines assigned to complete specific tasks while losing sight of their aspirations. It's a bit like treating team members as pawns on a chess board, when you reach the end game, they are critical to your overall strategy, but if you dismiss them early on or don't nurture them correctly right from the start, they won't be there to help when you need them most. This tendency is particularly prevalent when you're overwhelmed by the sheer amount of work that needs to be done, and personal development may seem like a luxury you can't afford.

It took me years to understand that people are still people; they still want to be treated like they are important and valuable, and that people perform much better at their jobs when they feel valued. Part of me somehow assumed that all individuality is lost once time is exchanged for money. Each party simply must deliver their part of the exchange, disregarding the human aspect of the relationship.

In my mind, I had to immediately present myself as the perfect leader when I agreed to step into that role. I did not allow myself to remain human, almost like putting on an imaginary 'leader hat' that had to magically transform me from someone who had just started her career into a seasoned and perfectly performing leader.

I was acting like a manager, managing mechanical components of a 'service output factory.' And completely neglecting the actual responsibilities of a leader.

Managing change

Managing change in a world where most people are looking for some security to hold on to is an extreme endeavour that should not be taken up by someone who has not even learned the basics of self-management in a leadership role. Managing change within an organization as a leader is like piloting a plane through turbulence. Just as a pilot must anticipate and navigate through unexpected air currents and unpredictable weather patterns (and maybe even flying wildlife) to reach their destination safely, a leader must manage the uncertainty and resistance that often come with organizational change, as well as metaphorical flying ducks!

Navigating turbulence while ensuring your team feels secure and comfortable is a skill you can acquire only through deep experience and empathy, together with inner knowing and trust that all is well in the organization.

I learned about this challenge by observing another young leader, Richard, who was put in charge of managing the takeover of our old and well-established business by a new, upcoming company. He had apparently swallowed a 'change-management-for-dummies' textbook and every Monday we were imbued with the words meant to coax a workforce, built on a century of tradition, into a modern-day productivity machine.

Although I could see the vision he so clearly presented in his MBA-inspired PowerPoint, I could sense his agenda's lack of authenticity and conviction. Managing change, I learned in this time, absolutely requires skill and expertise, and above all, honesty, integrity, and the ability to communicate in a way that invokes trust from the team.

Managing conflict

This is an essential aspect of a leader's role, and assuming it won't be challenging is unrealistic. Conflict is an inherent part of every workplace, and the greater the diversity of the workforce, the higher the likelihood of disagreements. We will be covering this topic in good detail later on.

Managing your team

Challenges will also vary depending on whether you were promoted from within the team or are new to it. If you were promoted from within, then managing the emotions and egos of your former colleagues and possibly even friends who now report to you can be challenging, as I experienced in my first leadership role. This dynamic can result in a toxic power struggle that manifests in subtle and overt behaviours such as eye-rolling, curt answers to questions, deep sighs (the passive-aggressive kind), and hushed voices when you enter a room.

In addition to this, building trust and respect may prove to be complicated if you are new to the team. You may encounter subtle subordination, such as team members 'forgetting' to execute tasks or making mistakes as an indirect way of showing you that they disagree with how you are doing things and are unlikely to cooperate.

I have come to understand these behaviours are mostly just these individuals dealing with change and their own feelings around that, in their own ways. But, when you are experiencing it first-hand, it will feel highly uncomfortable. This book aims to help you find ways through such situations.

Additional leadership challenges you may face

Besides the five most common challenges that leaders face, there are several other obstacles that you may encounter while on your leadership journey. Again, acknowledging these challenges and finding practical ways to tackle them will help you become a more competent and efficient leader, making your leadership journey less turbulent. Here are some additional challenges you may face, grouped into three categories, namely, communication, competency, and internal:

Communication challenges

Keeping everyone aligned to a shared vision and goal can be daunting, particularly if you do not fully understand or support the overarching vision and goal yourself. This challenge will be compounded when there is no clear objective other than making money or when there are no proper communication channels in the business.

When a team lacks alignment, it can feel like attempting to herd cats, continually correcting course, and micromanaging outputs that do not meet expectations. It is a frustrating experience, and it takes considerable effort to consistently guide people in the right direction, and you may envy other leaders with seemingly more competent teams. However, when you think along these lines, please take a closer look, as it may be a sign that you need to work on the alignment in your team and your own abilities as a leader. The fault is seldom with your team, and throughout the chapters in this book, you will learn how to master this skill.

Having honest conversations, especially when the topic is negative, can be an uncomfortable experience, made even harder when you have been promoted from within the team, and the person you need to speak with is a friend or former colleague.

Even when you understand that it is not personal and that you are expected to be capable of having these conversations with ease, it can be excruciating to speak to someone about something that may cause them embarrassment and discomfort or force them to confront unpleasant truths.

Celebrating success is often overlooked when the focus is always on achieving the next goal. I have learned from my time at a fast-growing startup that neglecting to acknowledge accomplishments can hurt the business and the people when, instead of taking the time to revel in the success of a completed project, the team is pushed to immediately shift their attention to the next goal, often causing team members to burn out from the gruelling workload, and to feel underappreciated and demotivated due to the lack of time for recognition.

Competency challenges

Making tough decisions is crucial, challenging and often lonely. Ben Horowitz aptly states in his book, "The Hard Thing About Hard Things,": *"Hard things are hard because there are no easy answers or recipes. They are hard because your emotions are at odds with your logic. They are hard because you don't know the answer and cannot ask for help without showing weakness."*

Often, you will find that employees do not appreciate or welcome the hard decisions, which can compound the challenge of making them. Don't be surprised if you feel isolated and resentful towards your team at times. For example, imagine you have just spent sleepless nights grappling with a decision, working tirelessly to arrive at the best possible outcome with the available information, only to face criticism and mistrust. We will cover decision-making in more detail in chapter 8.

Managing a business's resources. As a leader, your goal is to help the company achieve its objectives, including profitability targets. You will be acutely aware of the time and costs associated with each deliverable, and you'll also recognize how important it is to manage everything efficiently. The challenge lies in the fact that you will not always have all the answers, and often you will have to rely on incomplete information, making it difficult to make quick decisions; you may also overthink things in search of perfect solutions, further complicating matters. Now, imagine you have a strong team, eager and capable of assisting you, but they start questioning your ability to manage resources effectively, and you feel like you are losing their trust and support.

Delegating responsibilities is a delicate balance between micromanagement and trust. Learning to delegate effectively was one of the most significant challenges of my career because, as a self-confessed "control-freak" it always triggered instant fear within me. I naturally tried to do everything myself, believing nobody else could understand the work as I did, or do it the way it needed to be done.

However, this approach left me overwhelmed and overworked. Eventually, I would delegate some of the work, but often with tight deadlines that did not allow my team members enough time to do a good job. I would delegate with nervous energy, almost guaranteeing project failure. When the outcome was not up to my standards, I would use it to justify not delegating again, thinking that the team member could not perform the work satisfactorily. For me, this behaviour often led to a self-fulfilling prophecy, leaving unfinished projects and undervalued employees who felt their abilities were not appreciated.

Seeking feedback from others is a challenge many leaders face because they often value being right and having all the answers. This can lead to a fear of seeking feedback, as you fear hearing criticism or being seen as less than perfect.

The problem with this approach is that when you avoid feedback, you also deny yourself valuable opportunities for growth and improvement. Instead of shying away from criticism, seeking feedback can help you understand your blind spots and identify areas where you can improve.

Internal / self-related challenges

Some of the most limiting challenges I have experienced in my career were not from outside influences but rather related to my inner world of thoughts and feelings. These tend to remain unspoken for several reasons. One reason is the old perception that when it comes to the workplace, you are not supposed to show any emotions, and talking about how your own thoughts and feelings affect you is taboo because it portrays weakness. I often used to wonder how I was supposed to live in this dichotomy of being a complete individual in my personal life, considering my relationship with my loved ones, my community, environment, and spiritual self, all the while becoming the perfect one-dimensional replica of the ideal candidate in the role I need to fulfil in the workplace? By speaking out about the personal challenges I experienced, I hope to encourage you to admit and discuss the challenges you may also be experiencing so that you can function as a complete individual in business instead of putting on these role-related masks and suffering alone.

Staying positive when battling a flood of highly challenging concerns, from operational demands, management duties, and leadership challenges combined with self-doubt and potentially personal challenges, like health concerns, family situations, or relationship trouble, is not easy. When something is going on, making you feel down, be assured that your team will pick up on your state of mind very quickly. Most people are not fooled for long by fake smiles and pretend calmness. Some days, you may feel like you have nothing left to give, and all you want to do is roll up into the foetal position and cry, but this is not a luxury that an astute leader can afford openly.

Wanting to be liked is a natural inclination for most people; we are, after all, social beings, and not being liked and accepted by a group can lead to intense feelings of fear. There is a good reason for this, dating back to when we were cavepeople and much less autonomous. You see, with the technology you have access to today and the relative economic freedom you can create for yourself, you no longer depend on the social group you exist in to sustain your living as much. Still, your body remembers: back then, if you were to be an outcast from the group, you would most likely not survive. Your nervous system will likely have an intensive fear response when you experience disapproval from a group, which can happen easily when you make unpopular decisions as a leader.

Staying calm amidst chaos can be one of the most significant leadership challenges. I recall those feelings of nervous energy all through my body on the days in the office when things did not go right, and the job demands became overwhelming. Imagine you are the person trying to steer the ship in the right direction, but something in you is terrified of the ship capsizing because the waters are so rough. You get so focused on the crisis that your breathing becomes shallow, and you start feeling rigid and stiff. You scrunch up your shoulders, and you just get through the day. Your entire body goes into survival mode, and you cannot think past the next step.

Learning to trust your team members is an immense challenge for many of us, and I could never have imagined just how difficult this would be for me. When I first started leading teams, I had a deep-seated belief that no one could do the work as well as I could, so I almost begrudgingly entrusted tasks to the team when I realized that there was no way I had the bandwidth to handle it myself. When I didn't delegate at all, I became the bottleneck and would pause the entire production cycle when I didn't get to the things I needed to do, merely because I didn't trust anyone else to do it. I was afraid that I would be embarrassed or lose a client if I let a team member handle a task only to find out later that they did not do a good job, and in the worst-case scenario, I feared a client would complain about a job done less than perfectly. All of this led to micromanaging that created distrust and drove my team members to distraction.

Arrogance is another challenge that most leaders will encounter. None of us are immune to that feeling of being self-accomplished when we do a great job on a project or receive an accolade from a client or colleague, and maintaining humility as you succeed can be challenging. The trouble is that, in my experience, very few things can erode a team's trust as quickly as an arrogant leader who takes all the credit for the team's success. This causes your team to feel disconnected and disengaged.

Crippling fear can literally take away your ability to bring your best to your team. We all, from the most renowned leaders to the everyday person, experience occasional fear. From the fear of failure to the fear of upsetting your superiors and team or simply not doing well enough and disappointing a client. And these are only work-related fears. On top of that, you may have your everyday fears related to your health, your family, and your financial well-being. When you allow it, fear can creep in anywhere, and it can happen very quickly. It starts with a tiny thought that may sound like *"What if the client doesn't like the way we did this"* or *"What if there is a huge mistake on the quotation, and the final prices are wrong?"*. These questions lead to all kinds of worst-case scenario imaginations. Before you know it, you have manifested a full-blown fear response, unable to move forward and even less capable of leading the way and inspiring others. This response often leads to fear-based leadership, where threats of those worst-case scenarios are used to 'motivate' the team into action.

Inconsistency - Consistency and follow-through on commitments are key to building trust with your team and keeping team members motivated and enthused. This is, however, easier said than done. I recall a time when I was leading a small team, and we had established a very effective operation. We had found a good balance between feedback and review, and we were all working together quite well. Prior to this, I used to be the bottleneck, but with regular check-ins and consistent feedback, we turned things around. Things were about to change, though; the company had started the process of merging with another company, and an unexpected side effect was that I had to suddenly attend hours of management meetings every week, keeping me from my team and breaking the feedback cycle we had established. By failing to remain consistent and focused on my responsibilities to my team, I was causing harm to the environment of trust and enthusiasm we had built.

Anxiety and stress - Mastering the art of self-management during high-stress periods is one of the greatest leadership challenges I have faced, and it continues to challenge me in times of high workload and tight timescales. Managing anxiety and stress starts with self-care. I dedicate a morning self-care routine every day, where I commit myself to reading, journaling, meditation, and movement to keep me focused, clear-headed, and calm. The problems start when the demands on my time and energy mount (whether the demands be from family, work, or friends), and the first thing that goes out the window is my self-care routine to accommodate for the extra time needed for other obligations. Every so often (thankfully, it happens very seldom now), I find myself tired, cranky, and ineffective because I've compromised, leaving my body and mind so overwhelmed by the stressors that my lack of self-care allows my bucket of energy to run dry quite quickly.

What do stress and anxiety look like? It varies from person to person, but if you find yourself with shallow breath, feeling tired, having headaches, and the easiest telltale sign of all, having tight shoulders or a stiff neck, you are most likely experiencing anxiety and stress.

Anxiety and stress, when left unchecked, can lead to burnout, poor decision-making, and will cause harm to relationships with your teams, your clients and even your loved ones.

Demotivation can creep up on you without warning. We all have those days when we feel low, demotivated, and not in the mood to do anything, let alone lead anyone. For women, that can also relate to our natural monthly cycle. At certain times, we feel highly productive, and at others, we feel the need to retreat and move at a slower pace. We have stopped acknowledging these cycles over many decades by forcing ourselves to be productive, iron women every day of the month. Don't get me wrong, we are doing great, but the reality of our biology is that we will sometimes feel less inclined to make big moves and take bold decisions.

I remember the days of chastising myself for being lazy because I just could not get through my to-do list for a day or two. This is not unfounded because we are often pushed to do more and be more. On top of that, many of us have learned people-pleasing behaviours and patterns, leaving us feeling extremely guilty when we do not meet our own high standards of performance, leading to feeling like we have more weight on our shoulders and less self-motivation.

Disappointment is another grave cause of demotivation. It is difficult to keep your spirits high, never mind motivating a team, when you are processing a personal or professional disappointment. Imagine you are up for a promotion, or you have put immense effort into a personal project or relationship, and something happens that makes you feel like it was not worth it. You don't get the promotion, have a fight with your partner, or lose something of value to you. The natural reaction is disappointment, and we tell ourselves to 'get over it', knowing full well that it takes time, and, in the meantime, the show must go on.

Burnout is the absolute worst-case scenario, and hopefully, you will never get to this point. If you do find yourself on the brink of burnout, please do everything necessary to get well. How do you know if you have reached burnout? Here's how I knew: I had all the textbook symptoms, but I was too scared to let anyone else know.
I had been pushing hard to climb the corporate ladder for several years and I had no energy left. One day, during my lunch break - I found myself driving to a park near the office. I was not motivated to do anything, and I felt an immense sense of sadness and hopelessness. My life was good; I didn't feel like I had much to complain about (compared to many other people I knew at the time), but I still found myself in that car park, behind the steering wheel of my parked car, crying uncontrollably.

I felt huge guilt because not only was I slowing down my work pace as I physically could not keep up anymore, but I was letting down my clients and my employers, and my personal relationships were suffering too.

I felt desperate, lonely and above all, a fraud.

Feeling emotionally drained, overwhelmed, and stressed was my constant state. Physically, I was exhausted and felt run down all the time. I had lost interest in work and previously enjoyable activities like gardening, cooking, and socializing. My memory was letting me down as I constantly forgot things and couldn't concentrate for more than a few minutes. Irritable, cynical, and negative moods controlled me. Every night, sleep would evade me, and I was gaining weight because I started eating more for both comfort and to get some energy to get through the day. I experienced constant stomach pains and had regular health problems as my immunity took a knock, like a cold here and the flu there.

In short, it was a living hell. It took me months to speak out and tell anyone about what I was going through. I felt ashamed that I couldn't keep up and tried to hide it until I came to a complete standstill, realizing that this was my breaking point.

Maintaining human connection when you are being challenged by the work that you are doing, the deadlines are mounting, and you are just about holding it all together is not an easy feat. Taking the time to ask about your team's well-being, remembering what is important to them, and showing that you care about them on a human level is hard when every part of your being has been assaulted to problem-solve and approach challenges logically and systematically. Part of maintaining connection is vulnerability, which can seem near impossible when you are in 'fight' mode and facing a challenging time. In fight mode, we don't want to show vulnerability because that could let the opponent know where you are weakest. You can see how the opposing leadership requirements can trip you up here. On the one hand, you must be strong and confident in yourself, and on the other, you must show vulnerability in order to maintain human connection. It is a fine and challenging balancing act.

Self-doubt, that little voice inside your head that whispers into your ear that you cannot do this, you are missing a critical skill that you need to be successful, this is not your time, you are not ready yet. That inner critic can be mean and relentless, and we have all experienced it. It may differ for everyone, depending on your background, unique challenges, and insecurities. For me, it is that voice that tells me, midway through an important report, that I don't know what I am doing, that I am going to miss something big, and that I am going to be caught out for not being capable of the work I have been assigned to do. The thought of the absolute embarrassment and failure of that can leave me incapable of doing anything and can be counterproductive when you are trying to lead a team to greatness.

When Crisis Strikes

As a leader in crisis times, you will be faced with some of the most challenging and demanding situations in your career. You will have to navigate through uncertainty and make tough decisions, sometimes involving questions that challenge your value system, and more than ever, you will be expected to keep your team motivated and focused on achieving the organization's goals. The weight of your responsibilities can take a toll on your mental and emotional well-being, especially when the crisis is a threat to your own security.

Here are some of the greatest challenges I have faced in times of crisis:

Maintaining morale

I was the account manager heading up a large software tender team. I had invested all my and my team's time in a major bid that we were confirmed the front runners for and 95% certain to win. Until that one September morning, at 3 a.m., I saw an email in my inbox that would change the outcome completely. Everything we had been working on for six months that was due to start reaping rewards right about then had been canned. The client had a complete change of direction, and their company had found a way to remove the need for the software project entirely. It was an outcome I had not even considered, let alone planned for. I was devastated, embarrassed, and annoyed with myself that I hadn't seen it coming.

I lay awake for the next 3 hours, dreading the hour when the world would wake, and I'd have to face people. The Sales Director, my manager, was first; he saw the mail at around 7am, and I received the call, as expected. I had a glimmer of hope that he would have a solution, but he didn't. Sometimes there are no answers.

The real challenge came when I walked into the office that morning, knowing full well that within a matter of hours we would be sharing the bad news with the rest of the team. Although I was worried about the future of the account and barely got any sleep, I knew it was my responsibility to carry the team through this crisis. They would be looking to me for direction and next steps; how were we going to plug the huge gap in revenue that had suddenly appeared? I had to keep it together and keep them motivated.

Acting with clarity and honesty

In this same situation, it was an immense challenge to act with clarity and honesty. The situation was dire. The temptation to sugarcoat and paint a brighter picture than what we were faced with, was real. I did not want the team that we had spent years building and nurturing to dissipate and leave because of fear, and the idea of being left jobless if the business went down. I also knew deep down that I had to act with integrity. I had to be honest about the facts and the outlook. It was terrifying. I had no way of knowing how people would react but telling them something that wasn't true would be wrong. That was one of the harder days in my leadership journey.

Exuding calmness

At the same time as being honest and acting with clarity, I needed to exude calmness. As I have mentioned before, in times like these, the entire team will be looking at you as the leader to see if things are going to be okay. They will be feeling fear and uncertainty, the opposite of the safety and security that they need at a deep human level. This is one of the trickiest things to get right and one of those things that is very hard to fake. Human beings are hardwired to become hyper-vigilant when they are threatened so you will be observed very closely. Micro expressions and slight changes in your behaviour will be noted and interpreted by your team as they try to figure out whether they are safe sticking with you.

All of this is expected from you while you are in a state of worry, fear, and doubt. Being able to master your own emotions to be there for your team is the cross you bear when you choose to become a leader in business. This is where you will be tried and tested for strength and character the most.

You will learn ways to cope and excel, and as you develop your challenges will become more complex. This is part of the great work of a leader, to navigate your way through these rough waters and to emerge better and more competent on the other side.
There is, however, one challenge that surpasses all others that we have not mentioned. This is the number one challenge for the 85% of leaders who face this… what is the name of this

challenge, you may ask - it is called 'Imposter Syndrome,' and in the following chapters, we will look at this phenomenon in much greater detail.

Chapter 3 - It's the doubt that wins

"What a horrible thing to fail like that. I couldn't stand failure. Maybe they would all say I wasn't smart (clever) anyway."

- Gertrude Beasley,
My First Thirty Years

I walk into the boardroom, my palms are sweating, and my breathing is shallow. This is supposed to be a great new opportunity, I am excited to challenge myself, and now my body seems to be caving. The voices in my head are getting louder as more suited men (and a few women) walk in. I'm about to give a presentation that I had given many times before, very successfully, but today is different.

Instead of presenting to my peers or students, I am presenting to management. My mind is spinning with thoughts like, "am I good enough?", "What about that one slide that is not perfect yet, what if they hate it?", "What if they laugh at my ideas?", "What if it's too superficial?", "What if I have missed something important?".
But most of all: "What if they all realize that I don't know what I am doing?".

I can see them looking at me with judgment, I can already feel the potential discomfort of being asked questions that I don't know the answers to.

I can't shake the feeling that certainly they, these very sophisticated-looking and sounding people, cannot learn anything from me. Surely, I know that this is the end of the road for me. Is today the day I will be caught out for being a fraud, for being an impostor in a role and a world where I don't deserve to be?

I'd spend hours of my life wondering what it was about me that was just not good enough. Wondering what that feeling was that was eating away at my confidence and turning me, a strong, capable woman, into a nervous wreck unable to speak without a tremble in my voice and trembling hands.

Only years later, and to my great relief, I realized that I was not alone. The monster that I had been battling in my head that day, and many times after, goes by the name of "Imposter Syndrome". An apt name indeed as I found myself understanding the imposition it created in my mind.

I'm not typically a fan of labels and was baffled for a while by all the new ones that have sprung up in the last decade or so, however I do now appreciate that with the advent of Google and social media, having a label makes it far easier for people to search and find the support they need.

What is Imposter Syndrome?

"Imposter Syndrome", or the "Impostor Phenomenon", was first identified by psychologists Suzanne Imes, Ph.D., and Pauline Rose Clance, Ph.D., in the 1970s (we will refer to it as IS in the rest of this book). It is described as a condition that affects high achievers who struggle to accept their accomplishments and attribute their success to luck rather than their abilities. They often fear being exposed as frauds and suffer from anxiety and depression.

Although it is not officially recognized as a diagnosis in the DSM, many psychologists and professionals acknowledge that it is a very real and overbearing form of self-doubt that affects your intellect and ability to function. One of the scarier notions about IS is that those of us who experience these feelings tend to keep them to ourselves because we fear being discovered. You can see how this fear of being exposed, being the core fear of an imposter, can be unbearable for someone suffering from it to share, as voicing it might reveal the very "secret" that we are trying so hard to hide, that we are in fact, impostors.

It gets even worse if you work with someone who is also the person you would normally confide in, like a spouse or a partner. Imagine you are a parent, feeling like an imposter when it comes to parenthood, you cannot exactly share this with your partner out of fear that they may start seeing you and your abilities in a less capable light.

At its worst, IS can be extremely damaging: you may experience feelings of anxiety, an inability to accept and enjoy success, and in some cases, you may even believe that you cannot be successful and continue in your career. IS is characterized by a lack of confidence and the belief that you are incompetent, despite your achievements.

One of my classmates from college, Jessica, who was the top academic performer in our group, took a job at a local bakery, because she didn't think she would be able to do the work she had studied for well enough. It took me years to understand that Jessica had also suffered from IS. Throughout her interviews with potential employers, in stressful and judgemental situations, she felt like she was not equipped to add value to a world that seemed more sophisticated than she was ready for.

As PhD student, William Somerville put it: "There's a sense of being thrown into the deep end of the pool and needing to learn to swim," he says. "But I wasn't just questioning whether I could survive. In a fundamental way, I was asking, 'Am I a swimmer?'"

Imposter Syndrome is sometimes considered a cognitive distortion. Cognitive distortions are "the messed-up thinking that can get you stuck in negative emotions" as podcaster Neil Sattin calls it in an interview with Dr. David Burns, the author of "Feeling Good - The new mood therapy".

The theory around cognitive distortions says that you may have formed faulty or unhelpful thought patterns over time. This can result in not only doubting your abilities and accomplishments but also questioning your own history and track record, including the way others view you.

A look inside the mind of the imposter

let me introduce you
to a woman that I know
she hears my every thought
and follows everywhere I go

she wakes me up abruptly sometimes
when I'm fast asleep
and keeps me up for hours
whilst she taunts and laughs at me

she takes joy in convincing me
that I am hard to love
that if I'm less than perfect
then I'll never be enough

she shakes the ground I stand on
and talks down what I achieve
she highlights all my flaws to me
and tells me I'm naïve

she battles with my confidence
and wrestles with my pride
she's like a double agent
but she's never on my side

and she knows just how to sabotage
by sowing seeds of doubt
and arguing with logic
in a voice that likes to shout

and you'd think I wouldn't listen
that I'd turn and walk away
but it's so hard to ignore her
when she knows just what to say

in ways which make me question
things I've thought and done and said
you see, she's an imposter
and she lives inside my head

© 2022 "Sabotage" by Becky Hemsley
www.beckyhemsley.com

How do you know if you have Imposter Syndrome?

IS can be influenced by various factors, including standing out from most of your peers or assuming a new role or responsibility that you don't feel equipped to handle, leading to self-doubt when confronted with novel obstacles. Furthermore, IS is often linked with perfectionism, which can cause two typical reactions: putting off tasks or excessive preparation.

Do you ever feel that you are undeserving of your accomplishments and that the praise that comes with them is not meant for you? Do you often attribute your success to external factors like luck or good timing rather than acknowledging your abilities and your hard work? If you do, welcome to the club and be warned, IS is not merely limited to professional environments as you may think. It can also manifest itself in academics, personal achievements, play, and sports.

I recall a time in my younger days when I met up with some new work colleagues who had invited me to play a ball game with them one lunch time. I remember not having a clue as to what the rules of the game were but assumed I would pick it up along the way. It took only four words to disable me and invite the imposter to the forefront of my mind. Four little words which I overheard one guy say to the other *"she has no clue"*. I was horrified and left crippled. From that day onwards, I never played ball games. The voice in the back of my mind was ever present to remind me that I would either be found out for not understanding the rules or petrified of making a mistake again. As time went on, I gave up team games altogether and found no reason to willingly re-live the trauma every time I joined in. But life is not a ball game and I eventually realised that checking out is not that easy, because the imposter voice soon found new ways of tormenting me, in the workplace, in close relationships, and even in family life.

It's important to note that the imposter phenomenon can affect even the most driven personalities and individuals at the top of the career ladder. This suggests that professional success and confidence may not necessarily indicate immunity to IS and, in some cases, can exacerbate the issue. Perhaps it's because there is more pressure to perform when you have already had significant success, and you have come to rely on this success for self-esteem.

Many famous leaders have in recent years admitted to struggles of their own with IS. We mentioned Sheryl Sandberg earlier, Facebook's COO, who explains that she used to feel embarrassed whenever called upon in class or when she took a test, convinced she had underperformed. She also admitted to feeling that her successes resulted from fooling others and that she would eventually be exposed as a fraud.

It's worth noting that IS goes beyond occasional self-doubt and can be marked by persistent feelings of inadequacy, despite external evidence of success. While some self-doubt can be healthy, chronic self-doubt and the resulting self-sabotage can be debilitating. Experts agree that frequency is key in determining whether self-doubt has progressed into full-blown IS, which can significantly impact one's personal and professional life.

Tell-tale signs and Characteristics

If you think that you may be suffering from IS, you are probably right. Since it is extremely common and especially noticeable in people with high self-awareness. Someone like yourself, who is reading a book about IS, and who probably tends to be introspective to some degree, can be very susceptible.

If you are wondering whether you have it, here are a few telltale signs and characteristics that you may be displaying; if you answer 'yes' to more than two or three of these, you may indeed be suffering from IS:

- You experience self-doubt and feel anxious regarding your capacity to achieve success.
- Achieving success in work has become a goal that is fraught with risk and seems out of reach.

- You underestimate your contributions and the value of your accomplishments, leading to a persistent feeling of inadequacy.
- You credit your accomplishments to outside elements, frequently those that you cannot influence, and you don't acknowledge your role in your achievements.
- You are afraid of success causing you to believe that success is not attainable for you regardless of your efforts.
- You sabotage your success by making poor and risky decisions.
- You can undermine your abilities by convincing yourself that your contributions will be inadequate, sloppy, or pointless. If you start a project with these negative thoughts, you may not put in enough effort, attention, creativity, or persistence, which then reinforces those negative beliefs.
- You set impractical goals for yourself due to a belief that your utmost effort is inadequate, causing you to establish standards that are not feasible. You do so to make up for the feeling of incompetence even when achieving practical goals within a reasonable timeframe.
- You establish an unattainable and unsustainable level of performance for yourself, and not meeting this standard, triggers a sense of shame.
- Despite your best efforts, you are always afraid of not meeting expectations.
- You experience expectations as a burden rather than an exciting challenge.
- You experience burnout due to excessive self-imposed pressure and pushing yourself beyond your limits.
- You have lost your passion and feel a lack of a sense of purpose in your work because you have depleted your energy.

- You are restless and nervous, and you have negative self-talk.

Imposter Syndrome has many faces, and not everyone experiences it in the same way; in different phases of your life or situations, you may experience different 'symptoms' of this phenomenon. Let's look at the most common ways that people report their experience of Imposter Syndrome:

- **Anxiety** - Imposter Syndrome is often linked with different types of anxiety, such as trait anxiety, generalized anxiety disorder (GAD), and social anxiety disorder. According to experts, it is uncommon to see individuals with IS who do not exhibit some form of anxiety. This suggests that IS and anxiety may be closely related and require similar treatment and management approaches.
- **Self-Doubt** - The sense of self-doubt can be all-consuming and seep into every aspect of our lives, affecting relationships, careers, and the overall sense of self-worth. The inability to realistically assess your competence and skill is a common characteristic of IS. You may doubt your abilities and believe you are not as competent or skilled as others perceive you to be.
- **Fear of being exposed** - You may have a deep-seated fear of being exposed as a fraud, even though you have achieved objective successes in your personal or professional life. This persistent fear is often associated with a lack of confidence in your abilities. The fear of being "found out" can be all-consuming and can lead to chronic stress, anxiety, and even depression.
- **Giving away credit** - You may struggle to take credit for your achievements, even when you succeed. Instead, you may attribute your success to external factors such as luck, timing, or help from others. This tendency to downplay your accomplishments can

lead to feelings of relief or distress rather than happiness or pride.

- **Seeking validation** - You may need validation from authority figures, such as a boss, teacher, or family member. You may look to them to define what success means and feel that their opinion of you determines your worth.

- **Fear of disappointing others** - The fear of letting people down can lead to overworking or perfectionism to meet expectations. This often originates from a cycle of seeking external validation, where you may constantly seek feedback or approval from others rather than trusting your own judgment and feelings of accomplishment.

- **Berating your performance** involves being overly critical of yourself and your work, even when others may perceive it as successful or satisfactory. You might focus on your mistakes and flaws rather than recognizing your accomplishments and strengths.

- **Overachieving** - Overachieving means that you set excessively high expectations of yourself, even if you have already achieved significant success. You may constantly push yourself to do more, regardless of how much you have already accomplished, to avoid being seen as a fraud or failure. Overachieving can manifest in many ways, such as working long hours, taking on too much work, or setting unrealistic goals for yourself.

- **Sabotaging your success** – Another aspect of IS is a tendency to undermine your own achievements or avoid opportunities for advancement or recognition. You may feel like you don't deserve your success, driving you to engage in behaviours that prevent you from experiencing it, like leaving work till the last minute, making it impossible to achieve that deadline. You might avoid tasks that you believe you won't excel in, reject promotions, or not take credit for your accomplishments. Self-sabotage maintains the illusion that you are not good enough, which reinforces your belief that you are a fraud or an imposter.

How did I become susceptible to IS in the first place?

We have already mentioned that IS can happen to anyone under the right circumstances and with enough triggers. No one is immune to IS. However, certain early life environmental conditions can make you more susceptible to a bout of IS when you encounter such a trigger:

1. If your family valued achievement above anything else.
2. If you grew up in an individualistic culture with pressure to succeed and achieve (like the US).
3. If your family was characterized by low support and high conflict.
4. If you belong to a minority group.

I've already mentioned some of these in passing, now let's look at each of these predisposing factors in closer detail to gain a better understanding of why you may be suffering from Imposter Syndrome.

Please note that you may have a combination of any of these following factors, and whether you have only one or all four, the pain you are experiencing is equally valid.

1 - Your family placed an incredibly high value on achievement and success

I recall a day when my Mum finally attended one of my hockey games. I was just starting to do well in the sport and had my first real taste of success on the field. I remember feeling like I did well in the game; after all, we won shortly after I scored the winning goal!

I was excited to see my Mum's face and how proud she would be of me. That is something I did not see often. I ran up to her, still red in the face from the exertion, beaming from cheek to cheek with the euphoria of my victory. I asked her what she thought of my game, and she casually responded: 'Yes great, shame you missed that last one".

I recall the feeling that the comment gave me, my excitement disappeared, and suddenly I felt a bad feeling in my chest and in my stomach. I couldn't describe it at the time, but I can still feel it the moment I think of that story.

After that, I never really bothered with hockey again. I quickly lost interest and never considered why this shift had occurred. Today, I have a clearer understanding, realizing that the event made me feel like I wasn't a 'real' hockey player, despite the apparent success.

If your family placed an incredibly high value on achievement and success, you could be more likely to develop IS. Why is this? The theory is that growing up in an environment where success is important leads to internalizing the idea that your worth as a person is tied directly to your accomplishments. As a result, any perceived failure or lack of success can be deeply unsettling and leave you feeling ashamed and inadequate.

As if that is not enough, if you were raised in an environment where achievement is highly valued, you may tend to compare yourself to others and strive to be perfect, which contributes to IS, constantly feeling like you need to measure up to others and that any mistake is a reflection of your inherent value, creating a constant sense of anxiety and self-doubt because, where you grew up, mistakes and failures were not tolerated or accepted.

All of this can lead to a reluctance to take risks, as the consequences of making a mistake may be perceived as too costly.

2 - You grew up in an individualistic culture

Let's see an example of how our individualistic culture can contribute to your Imposter Syndrome. Take Mel as an example; she grew up in the United States, where personal achievements and accomplishments were highly valued from a young age. She (like other kids her age) was encouraged to be independent, assertive, and self-reliant. This sounds great in principle, right?

As she progressed through school, Mel received praise for her academic performance and extracurricular achievements. She was often compared to her peers and praised for doing better than the others in her class or team.

As she grew older and entered the workforce, she found herself in a competitive environment where, again, individual achievements were highly emphasized, and (to confuse matters) teamwork was also encouraged. She started feeling pressure to constantly prove her worth and demonstrate her competence above the team she was supposed to collaborate with. She was often praised for her successes, but she felt like she didn't deserve the recognition she received.

You see, because of the focus in her youth, on individual accomplishment, she could not ask for help because she was afraid of being exposed as an imposter and feared that others would think less of her if they knew she did not know how to do it all alone, a highly unrealistic standard when you are dealing with complex challenges that are best solved by a team with diverse experience and expertise.

When she did get the assistance of a team, and projects were successful, she would write the success down to the efforts of her team members and not any of her efforts, leading her, again, to the imposter category because, in her mind, the fact that she got help meant that she was too incompetent to do it herself.

3 - Your family was characterized by low support and high conflict

Growing up in a family with low support and high conflict can contribute to the development of IS. Experiencing lots of criticism and little validation when you do things will make you feel inadequate and insecure, especially in your formative years.

Did you constantly strive for your parent's approval and felt as though you never quite measured up? Did you experience lots of conflicts that made you feel stressed and emotional?

If you answered yes to either of these questions, you probably experienced more anxiety than you were meant to, and you've likely developed a fear of failure, a key component of IS.

The effect of this constant tension and uncertainty most likely led you to question your abilities. You end up feeling like you are constantly walking on eggshells, even years or decades after flying the family nest.

The environment described above is also most often hallmarked by a lack of emotional support and validation, making it difficult for young people to develop a strong sense of self-worth and confidence. As you carry this into adulthood, this will make you more susceptible to IS and you may have difficulty recognizing your achievements and talents.

4 - You belong to a minority group

This contributes to IS in several ways. First, members of minority groups may experience "Stereotype Threat," which is the fear of confirming negative stereotypes about your group. This causes self-doubt, feelings of inadequacy, and a sense of being an impostor.

Members of minority groups often face additional barriers and challenges in their personal and professional lives, such as discrimination and marginalization, leading to a feeling of not belonging and unworthy of their achievements. These experiences can exacerbate IS, as you feel you are only successful due to external factors rather than your abilities and accomplishments.

In addition, members of minority groups may lack role models and mentors who share a similar background to offer guidance and support, especially for young children.

When you feel like you don't belong in society, you start to feel isolated and think you don't deserve the new project, job, or title. Add to this the pressure to represent your minority group and excel in everything you do to disprove negative stereotypes, and you have a good recipe for IS.

Additional examples of experiences that may have made you susceptible to IS

While you may have underlying traits or experiences predisposing you to IS, as we have just discussed, there is usually a triggering event, a series of events, or the development of thought patterns or personality traits that may set you up for IS later in your life.

Below are some examples of the most common situations that can trigger Imposter Syndrome:

Over praising - Growing up, Emily's parents constantly praised her for being talented in art. This praise became a defining part of her identity, and she learned to associate her self-worth with her artistic abilities. As she got older and faced challenges in her art career, she started to doubt her talent and felt like a fraud whenever she received compliments on her work, fearing that she would be exposed as untalented and unworthy of praise. This is a great example of how over-praising parents can contribute to Imposter Syndrome. The pressure to maintain a label of being talented created self-doubt and a fear of being exposed as a fraud.

Controlling and overprotective parents - Carmen grew up with controlling and overprotective parents who rarely allowed her to take risks or experience failure for that matter. As a result, she struggled with self-doubt and lacked a sense of self-efficacy. Despite receiving praise for her achievements in school and work, she constantly felt like she was "faking it" and feared being exposed as a fraud. The lack of opportunities to develop autonomy and independence led to self-doubt and a constant need for external validation.

Being different from the group - Meet Debbie, a talented engineer who works in a predominantly male industry. She is the only woman in her team and, as a result, often finds herself feeling out of place. Despite her qualifications and abilities, she constantly questions her competence and feels like an imposter. As the pressure to conform to the male-dominated norms and expectations fell upon her, she started to doubt her abilities and question her legitimacy in the industry. Regardless of her skills and qualifications, she fears being exposed as fake or illegitimate in her work environment.

Constant comparison - Mark is a talented sales professional who works in a highly competitive environment. The company he works for strongly emphasizes meritocracy and achievement, and Mark has always been a high achiever. He values comparison and is constantly aware of how he stacks up against his colleagues in terms of sales performance. This mindset has helped him achieve success in the past, as he has often come out on top. However, Mark's reliance on comparison as a measure of his worth has also contributed to Imposter Syndrome. When he faces a setback or ranks below his colleagues' achievements, he starts to doubt his abilities and feels like a fraud, fearing that he is only successful when compared to others and not on his own merits.

Being in an environment where external achievements and accomplishments are highly valued - Melanie is a young professional who works in a highly competitive industry. She is part of a social circle where external achievements and accomplishments are highly valued, so she consistently feels the pressure to prove herself and meet the expectations of her peers. This social pressure creates a sense of anxiety and self-doubt, as the fear of being perceived as a failure or being rejected by her social circle if she doesn't meet the high standards, sets in. Regularly questioning whether her accomplishments are truly deserved, she works harder to maintain a facade of success to "fit in", leading to a cycle of self-doubt and fear of exposure.

Do any of these stories resonate with you? If so, this is even more of an indication that you may be dealing with IS. It is important to note that one person may experience a significant event, or as I called it in the above example, a 'triggering event', in an insignificant way, shaking it off or barely taking notice of any negative feelings, while the next person may indeed experience it as a triggering event for IS. This holds true not only for the early life experiences we looked at previously but also for certain personality traits that may make some of us more likely to develop Imposter Syndrome than others.

Personality make-up and IS

People with certain personality traits, like perfectionism and social anxiety, tend to be more likely to suffer periods of IS. Most of these behaviours are closely linked to dysfunctional thought patterns, as we touched on earlier in this chapter.

Below are some of the most common personality traits of people who suffer IS:

Perfectionism - As a woman, it's important to understand how perfectionism can contribute to IS. We often face societal pressures to meet unrealistic standards in various areas of our lives, including our careers, relationships, parenting, and appearance. Falling short of these expectations triggers a feeling of inadequacy and imposterism, making us question our abilities and accomplishments.

On top of societal expectations, we often also face gender-related biases and stereotypes that only add to our self-doubt. We feel the need to constantly prove ourselves in male-dominated fields and environments, leading to amplified perfectionistic tendencies and fuelling IS.

Neuroticism - Neuroticism is closely linked to IS. Take Mariana, for example, she has always been a highly neurotic person. She often feels anxious, insecure, and guilty about various aspects of her life and worries about making mistakes. This makes her feel overwhelmed by negative feedback or criticism, even if it is constructive. She tends to internalize the criticisms and dwell on her mistakes, triggering feelings of inadequacy and self-doubt. Despite her accomplishments and successes in her career, sadly, Mariana often feels like a fraud, believing that she does not truly deserve her achievements. High levels of neuroticism contribute to her constant emotional upheaval and intensifies her IS.

Social anxiety - Meet Katherine, a young woman who feels uncomfortable in social or performance-related situations, such as networking events or public speaking engagements. She worries about being judged or rejected by others and feels like she doesn't fit in with her peers. Social anxiety intensifies her IS, as she believes she lacks the confidence and ability to measure up to others, despite her achievements.

Introversion - Rhuda, is a talented and accomplished professional who happens to be an introvert. She often finds herself deep in thought, processing her experiences and reflecting inwardly. This introspective nature tends to ruminate on negative thoughts and self-doubt, particularly when it comes to her achievements and abilities. She internalizes feelings of pressure and failure, constantly striving for perfection in her work. Her introverted personality trait exacerbates her IS, as she relies heavily on her perceptions of her performance and abilities, which is often clouded by self-doubt and negative self-talk.

Events that may trigger IS

We have already spoken about triggering events in your early years and the development of thought patterns and personality traits that may set you up for IS later in your life. But a single significant event can also trigger the imposter in you.

Unexpected failure - can shake your confidence and leave you questioning your abilities and accomplishments. If you already have an underlying case of IS, experiencing failure can reinforce the belief that you are not good enough, that you have been fooling others into thinking that you are competent, and that you will eventually be exposed as a fraud.

Imagine you have achieved success in your field, and suddenly you experience a major setback or failure. Whether-it's losing a big client, a project not going to plan, or receiving negative feedback. Even though you have achieved success in the past, failure can cause you to doubt your abilities and feel like a fraud. You may begin to attribute your previous success to luck or the efforts of others, discounting your contributions.

Self-doubt spirals toward perfectionism, overworking, and self-sabotage to avoid future failure. The fear of being exposed as a fraud can be so severe that you may avoid taking risks or pursuing new opportunities for fear of future failure. Ultimately, the probability of limiting your growth and potential is high and perpetuates the cycle of IS.

Transitioning - While transitions can be a time of self-discovery and growth, they can also be a time of insecurity and doubt. Going through a transition, such as starting a new job or entering a new phase in life, can cause IS because the change creates new challenges and unknowns. The pressure to perform well in a new environment, combined with a lack of experience, can trigger feelings of inadequacy and self-doubt.

For example, there may be new tasks and responsibilities that you are not used to handling in a new job. You may be expected to learn new skills quickly and adapt to new work cultures. The pressure to succeed and impress your colleagues or superiors can be overwhelming. IS can set in quickly if you feel like you're not living up to expectations.

Similarly, when starting a new phase in life, such as going to college or starting a family, there are new expectations and challenges to face. In these situations, it's easy to feel like you're not equipped to handle the new responsibilities and IS takes control.

Bias and IS

Let's now look at how bias and social influences affect IS, as it has been found that discriminatory views, policies, and procedures towards people of colour and underrepresented populations can indeed worsen IS. When you experience differential treatment based on your race, socioeconomic class, religion, gender, or sexuality, it can lead to self-doubt, second-guessing, and stress.

I recall when I started my career back in the early 90s, working in the engineering industry. I decided to take up golf as a hobby. Back then golf was typically the domain of the businessman and not for females, but I felt that was where the big deals were being finalized and so I took a few lessons and even bought a half set of left-handed clubs, but after huge expense, the imposter within stopped me from ever going to play with any business colleagues or potential clients.

In addition to feeling 'out of place', some of you may feel like you don't belong in a role because of **tokenism**, you may set higher standards for yourself to prove that you deserve the position and to break the stereotypes of the group.

The prevalence of IS and why it matters

People hide IS, they push through the pain because they feel like they do not want to admit imperfection or vulnerability. When the workplace is very competitive and there is a tendency to be non-accepting of imperfection, the situation can become dire and harmful to individuals predisposed to this syndrome. Let's take a closer look at how IS can affect your life, when left unchecked.

The impact of IS

Suffering from IS pushes you to strive for success, but the cost is constant anxiety. You over-prepare and work harder than necessary, just to make sure no one discovers that you're a fraud. Unfortunately, this anxiety worsens over time and may eventually lead to burnout and depression.

It creates a vicious cycle where you believe that the only reason you succeeded in the first place, was because of your over-preparation, leaving you feeling like you don't deserve to be where you are and when you do accomplish something, the nagging feeling of being a fraud doesn't go away. This can be especially difficult to navigate if you have received early feedback stating that you weren't good in social or performance situations.

These negative beliefs result in a lack of motivation, difficulty making decisions, low self-esteem and self-confidence, emotional instability, and procrastination. The problem is that even when you do well, you brush it off as luck and this constant self-doubt harms your work performance and quality of life.

This pattern can be repeated several times in cycles of over-performing followed by burnout, and this is unlikely to stop, unless you get to the root of the problem, your IS.

Imposter Syndrome (IS) FAQ

After establishing the basics of IS and its origins, it's worth exploring some frequently asked questions about the phenomenon before diving into its various types. By doing so, we can gain a more comprehensive understanding of this psychological phenomenon and the impact it has on people.

Question 1: How common is IS?

IS is a relatively common experience, affecting a significant percentage of high achievers and adults. According to research, about 23-30% of high achievers have experienced IS. Additionally, it is estimated that around 70% of all adults may experience IS at least once in their lifetime.

Question 2: Can you be diagnosed with IS?

IS is not recognized as an official psychiatric diagnosis in the DSM, so you cannot be officially diagnosed with it. However, the feelings and experiences associated with IS can lead to other conditions like anxiety and depression, which can be diagnosed and treated by mental health professionals.

Question 3: Are women more likely to experience IS?

A study shows that 50% of female and 31% of male managers experience self-doubt regularly. In addition, a KPMG study found that 75% of female executives across industries have experienced IS in their careers. These statistics suggest that IS affects both men and women, but may be more prevalent among women, particularly in leadership roles. Women may also put more pressure on themselves not to fail than men do, which can contribute to feelings of inadequacy and self-doubt.

Question 4: When is it humility and when is it IS?

Humility and caution come from an honest evaluation of one's abilities concerning a complicated situation, whereas the imposter phenomenon arises from a feeling of incompetence in the situation despite having the skills to be competent. The distinctive aspect of IS is that it is not about evaluating the situation but rather evaluating yourself. When you have IS, you feel more inadequate than others facing the same complex situation, so much so that you believe you don't belong there.

Types of IS

IS is not a one-size-fits-all experience. It comes in different varieties, with a focus on different manifestations of the syndrome and nuances in how it is experienced by different individuals in various circumstances. Experts have organized the occurrence of IS into 5 different types, which we will describe in detail in the paragraphs below. It is essential to keep in mind that you may have characteristics of different types, or you may be very representative of one type. This method of delving deeper into IS is an attempt to recognize your individual experience more accurately and describe it as an easy point of reference, keeping in mind that there may be many more variances based on your individual experience.

The Perfectionist

Perfectionist types have an insatiable hunger for success, always striving for better outcomes and higher prestige. Despite achieving ambitious goals and putting in a lot of hard work, you still feel unsatisfied. Your fear of losing control is what drives your perfectionist behaviour.

Perfectionists often set extremely high expectations for themselves and struggle with self-acceptance when they fall short. You tend to focus on small imperfections and mistakes, which can lead you to feel like a fraud even when you are successful. This feeling of inadequacy and anxiety can result in procrastination or even avoidance of tasks to prevent the possibility of failure.

If you are a perfectionist type, you may also struggle with delegation and collaboration because you probably believe that you are the only one capable of doing the job correctly, leaving you overworked and overwhelmed, resulting in burnout. The constant pressure you put on yourself to be perfect can also cause you to experience physical and emotional symptoms of stress.

The Superhero

The Superhero type of IS sufferer is characterized by a constant need to do more in less time. You may be a Superhero if you thrive on the feeling of validation that comes with working overtime and proving your ability to handle any task thrown your way. The fear of having free time or seeking personal fulfilment outside of work is what drives your behaviour. You constantly work harder than your peers to prove your worth and mask your imposter feelings.

When you are a Superhero you measure your competence based on the number of roles you can juggle and excel in, and you feel like an imposter when one area of your life is not as strong as the others. This behaviour can quickly lead to burnout and take a toll on your physical and mental health.

The Natural Genius

The Natural Genius is the imposter who feels like a fraud because they believe their success is solely based on innate talent or intelligence. If this is you, you may feel that you must get things right the first time, every time. When you get feedback or criticism, this will devastate you because it feels like a threat to your belief in your natural abilities.

If you are a Natural Genius imposter, you may put in minimal effort and often still succeed, and this can lead to feelings of guilt and shame because you don't believe you truly earned your success.

The Rugged Individualist

The Rugged Individualist is an imposter who believes that they must achieve success entirely on their own, without any help or support from others.

If this is you, you may see asking for help as a sign of weakness and vulnerability, which makes you feel uncomfortable and exposed. This can make you feel inadequate as you struggle to live up to your own expectations of being able to do everything independently.

The Expert

The Expert is an imposter who focuses on having complete knowledge and experience before taking on any job or task. The fear of inadequacy is the underlying emotion here, as you feel like you must know everything, and anything less is considered a failure. This obsession with knowledge and expertise can lead you to a vicious cycle of anxiety, self-doubt, and over-preparation, causing a delay in taking action or completing tasks.

This constant need to be an expert creates unrealistic expectations for yourself. It can lead to feelings of shame and failure if you fall short, which is bound to happen at some point, and you cannot possibly be an expert at everything you do right from the beginning.

The Noticer

The Noticer is always looking for mistakes and flaws in their work, constantly critiquing and self-evaluating. No matter how much you achieve or how successful you may be, you cannot take pride in your work, as you always find some fault in it. Even when a project is completed successfully, you feel relieved that it is over instead of feeling proud of your accomplishments.

As a Noticer, you will also be acutely aware of your competition, and you may compare yourself to others, always feeling like you are a step behind. The underlying emotion for this type of imposter is the fear of not belonging - not being good enough to fit in or to be accepted by others. This fear drives constant self-criticism and the inability to take pride in your achievements.

The Discounter

Do you tend to dismiss evidence of your competence, talent, and recognition? Does it feel as if, no matter how much you achieve or how many accolades you receive, you constantly discount your accomplishments as a fluke or downplay your contributions to a project or task? The Discounter knows this all too well and undervalues their abilities and achievements.

A Discounter tends to undervalue support systems, too, whether it be colleagues, friends, or family. You may brush off compliments or accolades, feeling like you don't deserve them or that others are just being kind. The underlying emotion for this type of imposter is a fear of not being good enough, which can lead to a lack of confidence and self-doubt.

* * *

So, now that we've seen what IS is, and you may have realized that indeed you suffer from it yourself, you may be asking *"How can I combat this Imposter Syndrome?"*

In the rest of this book, we will look at the solutions. There are two ways to combat IS, and it is best to use both if you are serious about winning the battle – one is directly tackling the internal thoughts that make you feel like an imposter (including specific thought patterns that are unique to the different types of IS), and the second is through self-care, and focusing on your growth with strong foundations – especially since it is your job-related achievements that may bring about IS.

As I said, these two paths aren't options, you need to do both, so with that, let's look at how you can take charge of those unhelpful thoughts.

Chapter 4 - Silencing the Challenger

---

*"In the inner courtroom of my mind, mine
is the only judgment that counts."*

- Nathaniel Branden,
Six Pillars of Self-Esteem

Overcoming IS

Let's rewind back to my nightmarish boardroom experience.
The presentation to my management team, one of my earliest
memories of a full-blown episode of IS, the voice in my head
ringing louder and louder, *"... is today the day I will be caught
out and cast aside?"*

Living through an episode of IS, as I did, is hard, and while it
is helpful and somewhat soothing to know that others are in
the same boat, it does not take away the fear. Once you have
accepted your self-diagnosis of IS, what can you do to improve
things and feel better?

IS is a complex condition, as you know by now. Having read
this far, you know that it stems from a variety of contributing
factors, and it can be triggered in many ways, often hitting you
unexpectedly. Due to the nature and complexity of its
formation, there is no easy fix, and there is no 12-step program
to work through (that I know of, at least). As with most personal

healing, it takes dedication, persistence, and focus to rescue yourself from the personal hell that IS can cause.

This being said, the reward will be sweet. Imagine a day when you can show up fully aware of your abilities, your limitations, and your true value—the day when you can confidently claim your victories and consciously admit your defeats. When failures do not devastate and derail you any longer, every problem becomes an opportunity for growth, not only as a leader but as an ever-evolving conscious and boundless individual.

I wrote this book to tell you about the solutions I have found over the years. Some of the tactics and tips I share will work for you, and some you will resist. I encourage you to try all of them, even when you get uncomfortable. IS effectively requires a holistic strategy and continuous commitment to wellness.

Let's now look at how you can take the first steps to gain control of your life and stop that nagging feeling you have that any mention of your thoughts would make you seem somehow ungrateful for your life and any success within it.

Ask for help and change your thinking

Talk to your mentors

Part of the experience of IS is that you are afraid that you will be found out, so it is easy to understand why most people with IS will suffer in silence. When you're able to, step outside of this fear and tell a mentor about your feelings so that they can constructively support you. As they are looking in from the outside of your situation, they can see it more objectively, they will be able to point out where your thinking may be distorted, and where you may be irrational. They can also help to keep you in check where you may be sabotaging yourself.

Recognize your expertise

A great technique to build your self-confidence and learn to trust in your abilities is to establish yourself as an expert. This changes your perspective and helps you feel more secure. When you teach others, a feeling of pride spreads through your being, even more so as you watch them gain an understanding and succeed, leading you to experience an increased feeling of accomplishment when you see the outcomes of your teachings. In this way, teaching becomes a powerful self-healing tool. I experienced this myself in my first professional role; becoming an educator in my field enhanced my perception of my abilities and that was reinforced every time I was able to teach someone else.

Remember what you do well

It's worth noting that sometimes it's not IS; sometimes you are just a little (or a lot) out of your depth, and there is a substantial amount of work that needs to be done to get you upskilled enough to perform at the level required in a situation. You need to acknowledge this, and while it is by no means easy, it must be done because, without this self-evaluation, you will always wonder whether it's IS or just your incompetence and underdeveloped skill. Your mind will play tricks on you and make you doubt yourself.

Practically, you can create a personal "evidence list." An Evidence List is a document that contains two columns. One column should list your competencies and the other your inadequacies. Update this as time passes to help you stay grounded and rational about where you are the imposter and where you truly need to improve your skill set. Allocate some time, every week if you can, to rate your skill and knowledge levels for each item on your list on a scale from 1-10 (one meaning 'I should not be doing this at all, I'm dangerous", and 10 being "I know how to do this with my eyes closed"). This list will become your benchmark for silencing the attacker in your mind when it's not being fair to you.

This kind of honest appraisal helps you to check yourself in each situation. It will help you determine if you are having an episode of IS, or whether you are in a situation where you need assistance and you still have some things to learn. It is important to be very honest and realistic when you do this exercise, otherwise, this exercise becomes one in positive thinking, which will not be helpful in those moments of deep self-doubt.

Realize no one is perfect
To beat the effects of IS, it is non-negotiable that you must launch a fully-fledged war against perfectionism. I find in myself and the leaders around me that some of us still secretly wear our perfectionism as a badge of honour. Why do we do this?

I remember when I had my first career coach, and I asked him what I should say when I was asked about my greatest weakness. The advice he gave me was that I should admit to a weakness that will benefit my potential employer and can be seen as a strength as well. The go-to answer to that question became that my greatest weakness is my perfectionism.

For years, no decades, I secretly felt proud of my perfectionism. But, once I came face to face with some of the worst effects that IS can have, (burnout, depression, deteriorating health, relationships, and plummeting work performance), I realized that I could no longer afford to hold onto that tainted belief and the impossible standards I was setting for myself.

If you are serious about beating IS, you must change the fundamental belief that trying to be perfect is desirable.

How do you do this when it has been ingrained so deeply? Allow yourself to accept small mistakes, look at the bigger picture instead of zooming in on mistakes as perfectionists tend to do, and remind yourself that 75% is good enough.

One of the most empowering pieces of advice I have ever received is to do every task well enough. Everything does not have to be perfect; every piece of work does not have to be a masterpiece and expecting that of yourself does not benefit you or anyone else (whether it is your boss, client, or spouse). Holding yourself to that standard will eventually lead to burnout and a loss of productivity, at which point you will not have much to offer, and it may take you weeks, even months, to recover.

Can you accept "good enough" as good enough and stop insisting on perfection?

Change your thinking
Some call the distorted thinking of IS "Superstitions" or "Belief Patterns." What are your superstitions? What beliefs do you have that could be detrimental to your mental health? I have seen all kinds of superstitions, like: *"I have to work all night to get this done," "I must spend at least 10 hours on that", "No one can see my work before it is perfect," "I must work really hard before this will be acceptable."*

To change your thinking, you must challenge your thinking. There are different techniques that you may use to challenge your thinking, which we will go through later in this book. The changes will be incremental. At first, you may feel like it is not working, but consistency over time will bring about the transformation you are looking for.

Talk to someone who can help
Talking to a professional can help you dissolve your IS. Make sure that you find a therapist who is familiar with IS, and who understands how to work through the imposter feeling and empower you to feel better in the long run. Getting

professional help is easier today than it has ever been, and much of the stigma has thankfully been removed.

Warning - Don't always follow conventional wisdom

When it comes to managing IS, especially in the workplace, conventional modern-day wisdom and advice may not serve you. Instead, it can end up hurting you, especially if you are a first-time manager and you lack experience and the strategic knowledge to navigate workplace politics. Advice like *"Be vulnerable"* and *"Don't take credit where you can pass it on to your team"* has the potential to cripple your career efforts.

Let's take an example of a project I worked on some years ago. About one month into the project, I realized that I did not have all the skills that were expected of me, namely that I knew nothing about contract law. I was assured in the interview process that I didn't need any specific skills beyond the ones clearly indicated on my CV and a good connection with the team. Although I was intimidated by the prospect of working for this client, a giant multinational corporation, I trusted this information in the interview and took the project head-on.

Once I realized I did not, in fact, have all the skills I needed, I had no idea what to do. I found myself stuck between a rock and a hard place. I believe in a policy of honesty and transparency, yet instinctively I knew that sharing my budding insecurities would not be good for me or my career.

Let's look at a few pitfalls of conventional wisdom that you will do well to avoid:

Be cautious about showing vulnerability
I have mentioned in the first two chapters of this book several times that modern leadership requires connection, and one of the ways to build a connection is through being vulnerable.

This stands true, but there is an important exception. Showing vulnerability in the core competency that you were hired for, which is expected of you, can cause all sorts of havoc, and can make you appear weak, making you an easy target for discrimination.

When your team gets a whiff that you are doubting your own management skills, the results will usually not be positive. Be very cautious before choosing this course of action; in fact, I do not recommend it at all. While it is commendable to admit mistakes and show your human side, your team will not be able to confidently follow your lead if you openly admit doubt in your abilities.

In my project, it would not have been wise to inform my line manager, who was already clearly stressed about the project and how the results would reflect on her and impact her career, that I did not really know how to do all that my job required.

You will have to find someone outside of your team or your business to help you through this. Unless you have a mentor, you can trust, and who is not a boss, employer, or team member, I recommend getting a professional counsellor to assist you. If that is not possible for whatever reason, find someone outside of your business network that you can call on for support. You could also get a career coach, a support group, or both. Build a solid network of people to support you.

When you find yourself in this situation, ultimately, your choices will be to either skill up or step down. Do an honest evaluation of your abilities and decide which path is ultimately the best for you and your career.
We will take a closer look at this a little later.

Recognize your contributions - there is an 'I' in everything, including "team"

How can you build a genuine sense of how your contributions affect outcomes if you cannot be honest about the positive (and negative) contributions that you make? We have been taught to give credit to the team, and while it sounds righteous to do so, when you do this to the point of negating your efforts and expertise, you are devaluing yourself not only in your eyes but in the eyes of your peers and teams, too.

Instead, I recommend taking time to do an honest and healthy appraisal of your efforts and their effects, followed by owning the result in a firm and humble manner. Even in cases where your team did all the 'work,' it is crucial to identify and acknowledge your role in making that happen.

I have often received these wise words: "Humans are just humans," and if you tell someone enough times that your efforts or contributions to a successful project are negligible, they may just start to believe you.

Ask for affirmation

When you feel like you have done well, it is perfectly okay to ask for feedback that is positive and specific. Remember that in a business, especially a business where things move fast, and there are many crises and problems to sort out every day, mistakes are often recognized and highlighted because they require attention and need to be fixed swiftly. The trouble with this is that when things go right, it tends to go unnoticed. Asking for positive feedback will help you get a handle on IS, and it will also serve as a real-life reminder of your value to the person giving you the feedback.

Make sure that you get specific feedback by asking guided questions, such as asking for three things that you did in the last quarter that had a positive effect on the business.

Platforms like LinkedIn also have really simple tools built-in to request feedback in the form of "Recommendations" from both clients and colleagues.

Be honest about where you are

The truth is that sometimes you just don't know what you are doing, like me in the previous example. That is okay. It happens. Every new job has a learning curve, and it is impossible to know everything from the get-go. How do you deal with this? Firstly, you must be honest. In previous steps, I spoke about doing an honest assessment of your skills and your performance. Take an in-depth look at yourself and recognize and accept where you are limited and imperfect, it will be one of the most freeing activities you do this week.

As mentioned before, in the workplace, you should be cautious of who you share your insecurities with; start by being honest with yourself, and then share this with your trusted support network.

If you do choose to carry on with the task at hand, you'll have to do the leg work necessary to improve yourself and your shortcomings in the situation. Powering through and doing the work is a positive way of dealing with IS. Going into a negative spiral of self-doubt is not.

Even if today, you can only have confidence in your ability to learn to get better, that is a much better approach and position to be in than spinning into a full-blown episode of IS.

A seven-step approach to combating IS

Some of us work best with a methodical approach to solving problems, so here is a simple seven-step process that you can use to combat your inner imposter whenever you recognize her. What is great about this method is that it deals with all the different types of imposters:

Step 1 - Use the Coué Method

The Coué method will help you change how you talk to yourself and can then change your feelings, thoughts, and the way you act. It consists of 4 tasks:

- Choose an affirmation that opposes the imposter voice in your head, something like "I've got this."
- Find a safe space, whether that is a pillow in the corner of your room or a space in nature, whatever you can manage.
- Create an image in your mind that represents the affirmation you picked, a symbol, if you will, something like a dragonfly, a hawk, or a flower; anything that resonates with you.
- Now close your eyes, repeat your chosen affirmation to yourself (you can do this quietly in your mind if you have an audience, and simultaneously visualize your symbol).

Doing this for a few minutes, at least twice a day, helps you combat the feelings of imposterism, and it will get easier and easier to believe your affirmations.

If you get negative thoughts popping in, thoughts like "I am not good enough" or "I can't do this," just take note of the thoughts and refocus on your affirmations. Whatever you consistently repeat to your mind, it will eventually believe.

Step 2 - Journaling

Whatever the underlying troubles and traumas are that cause your IS in the first place will eventually surface and must bo addressed if you want to get rid of IS for good.

Journaling is a very simple way to start doing this. Grab a journal and a pen and start writing down everything that you are and have been trying so hard to hide. Ensure the privacy of your journal by keeping it safe and out of reach to other people. Journaling on an electronic document on your computer, with a password only you know, is also a good solution.

A simple task like this will take a weight off your shoulders. Moving some of these feelings from inside your mind onto paper opens a space inside yourself to fill it up with helpful thoughts and feelings that will serve your best life.

You can also verbally express yourself and talk to someone about the feelings you wrote down if you have someone you can trust. Talking to a therapist can also help you work through your challenges to get well.

Step 3 - Go for the small wins

I would like to challenge you to start taking on more risks because, even though risks may feel counterintuitive to you, when you succeed, you get a 'winner's rush', a dopamine flood through your brain that makes you feel good. We have all heard the saying, "Success breeds success," and this is a great way to anchor that success feeling.

It's critical to also capture your wins; recording your success in a journal is a great way to do this. I keep my 'Success Journal" separate from my 'Fear Journal.' You could also use the back of a book for your fears and the front of the book for your wins if you want to keep it all together.

Step 4 - Keep a success file

This may sound a bit extreme, but why not do whatever you can to take charge of your mind and your life? It does not have to be a big lever-arch file; you can simply write some notes of gratitude on your phone or take screenshots or photos of things you are grateful for and that make you feel that success vibration or feeling in your body. Save it in a folder called "success file" for ease of reference.

Do this for small wins and proud moments, and soon enough, you will have a file full of "evidence" portraying your extraordinary abilities. Store anything that you find uplifting and add it to your file. Include things like awards and compliments, too.

Remember to make time every so often to look through your success file; this will help you feel good about yourself and help prevent those downward spirals.

Step 5 - Go on a digital detox

Social media is a great way to compare yourself to others and to feel horrible about yourself if you feel that you don't measure up to the picture-perfect, mostly photoshopped images of your favourite influencers and fancy friends.

Why not give yourself a break? Human beings existed without social media for ages, you don't need it to survive, and you will probably thrive by taking a timeout.

Do this twice a year for ten days, and you will give yourself a mental wellness head start just like that. If you can get off emails at the same time and allow yourself a complete digital detox, that will be first prize.

Step 6 - Use the power of yes

Say "yes" to more challenges that feel good to you. The caveat is that you must say yes to things you want; no people-pleasing yeses allowed here! Ensure you don't overburden yourself with responsibilities (a constant trap for fellow IS sufferers), but say yes to adventure, life, and challenges whenever it feels right.

If the only thing stopping you from saying yes is fear, why not consciously kick that fear for the moment and take on the challenge? It could lead you to surprising places.

Step 7 - Set reasonable goals

Finally, decide that from this day forward, you will set more reasonable goals for yourself. How do you do this? Firstly, be honest with yourself and take a moment to think before committing to deadlines or announcing a goal.

Ask yourself, am I trying to please someone? Will I be able to do this without letting something else slip? Did I leave some time and space for the unexpected? Be honest and set attainable expectations. It is much better to under promise and overdeliver than to make commitments followed by excuses. In fact, this is something you absolutely want to avoid, as it will awaken feelings of imposterism in you.

The SBNRR Technique for dealing with IS

IS is a form of self-sabotage, and you are not helpless against this saboteur inside yourself. But do not try to ignore it. Instead, tame the emotion by acknowledging its presence and beware of its impact on your body.

The SBNRR technique (stop, breathe, notice, reflect, respond) can help you slow down and consider the situation — and your thoughts, feelings, and reactions — more mindfully.

Here's how to do it:

Stop: Allow yourself to stop in your tracks and take a moment to pause. Close your eyes if you can.

Breathe: Give yourself a deep breath and let your thoughts go, consciously letting go of your attachment to them. You can even imagine thoughts as balloons and release them into the sky, one by one or a whole bunch at a time.

Notice: Notice your feelings, your body sensations, your surroundings, people around you, the situation, what is happening, how you are reacting, and take in anything else that appears to you.

Reassess: Now, evaluate the situation as objectively as you can. The aim is to find that trigger, the reason, or the thing that made you fall into IS.

Respond: React intentionally from your new perspective of understanding why this is happening, and you will notice how you are calmer, more rational, and kinder to yourself.

Every time you go through this exercise, you will strengthen your 'imposter resistance'; it will get easier and easier, and you will feel better and better each time.

The IS Toolbox

IS originates from your thoughts and works by distorting them, basically turning your mind against itself. It can be extremely painful and tough to get it under control. When you cannot trust your mind, coupled with the inability to escape it, not even for a moment, it causes an array of negative effects within your body, relationships, and work. In essence, every single area of your life can be impacted.

We've already looked at several ways in which you can manage, and fight IS, but these won't fit every situation, every time. Every person is different, and every situation has its unique challenges and related feelings. You need a range of tools to deal with this complex condition. Therefore, I want to give you all the tools I know to assist you in your quest. Play around with them, and over time, you'll develop your own personal 'toolbox' that works for you.

1. Learn to understand the voices of the saboteurs in your head

We have hundreds of thousands of thoughts every day. Some of them we call positive thoughts, and some we label negative. When experiencing an acute phase of IS, the voices become saboteurs, threatening to cause real-world damage in your life.

Have you ever experienced this? The feeling that your head is spinning with thoughts. One after the other, mean, critical, unhelpful thoughts? It becomes hard to manage and drains your energy, gets you nervous, and eventually, you're left feeling down, tired, and even depressed.

Understanding the familiar voices makes it easier to identify what is happening, and it becomes easier to manage the thoughts. Here are some of the more familiar voices you may experience.

The Judge: She is the 'master saboteur,' the one everyone hears. She will beat you up, remind you of your shortcomings and failures, and make you think about everything that could go wrong, leaving you worried, critical, stressed, and generally unhappy with life. You become ineffective and unproductive, and your relationships will suffer, too.

The Judge operates very effectively on her own but sometimes brings in her accomplices, making things even worse. Here are some of her favourite helpers:

The Avoider is recognized by her sunny disposition, always focusing on pleasurable things while failing to complete unenjoyable tasks and difficult conversations.

The Controller always needs to be in charge and tends to control others. Her nervous energy and impatience make her easy to identify when she doesn't have control over situations.

The Hyper-Achiever relies on achievement and performance and needs this to feel self-respect, valued, and validated. Of course, she doesn't recognize or enjoy her achievements, always chasing the next high.

The Hyper-Rational voice is always processing and rationalizing everything. Constantly analysing situations, including human relationships, makes her appear cold and arrogant in her intellectualism.

The Hyper-Vigilant voice exhaustively looks out for anything that can possibly go wrong. Day in and day out, she never takes a rest.

The Pleaser is a well-known one, always helping, fixing, flattering, and, of course, rescuing. She eventually becomes resentful because she always puts others first and neglects to take care of her needs.

The Restless one always looks for the next adventure, distraction, or something to do. She is never content with the moment.

The Stickler holds a very high standard and needs things to be perfect. Anxiously organizing and reorganizing all the time in an attempt to make constant improvements.

The Victim, or the martyr, is emotional and temperamental, with laser focus directed on painful feelings.

2. Take time to evaluate what you value

Refocus your attention away from the signs of success in the outer world and connect with what makes you feel successful inside yourself. Maybe you do not value those work accomplishments as much as you 'should,' and you value your friendships and the positive impact you have in your community more. Take note and incorporate it into your schedule, allowing you to spend your time and energy on what you value most.

3. Reframe around growth

Challenge yourself; you are on a journey that will likely stretch over decades; your life and career will change over time, and there will be ebbs and flows. Keep stretching yourself. Humans were designed to want progress; give yourself those opportunities to grow and succeed. When you fail, keep reminding yourself that you are learning and growing, and instead of ruminating on negative thoughts, take action to improve where you need to and get real about where you are doing well enough.

4. Get out of your head

Do something physical. Take a walk in nature, play a game, or stretch your body. Remember that you are not your thoughts, and you can and should take charge of your mind. You do not need to be a slave to your negative thoughts.

You have probably heard the saying, "Get out of your head and into your body". I love this saying because it makes a world of difference when you are in a negative space. For me, "getting into my body" requires something physical that is quite rigorous. A gentle stroll, for example, will just see me ruminating while walking. Better than worrying on the couch, but not quite life changing. Going for a bike ride or a core yoga class, however, takes me out of my head as I use all my resources and energy to focus on the physical challenge. It is liberating when you learn how to make this shift.

5.   Have empathy with yourself

Don't be so hard on yourself for having IS. It was cultivated in your being over years and years, most likely starting when you were a defenceless baby or young child. Acknowledge this and keep using the techniques you are learning to get better. You've got this.

6.   Be kind...to yourself

How often do you tell yourself that you should be kinder to others? How often do you forgive others for mistakes and oversee their flaws? If you are like most people, you do this all the time for friends, family, co-workers, and kids. Why not show this same kindness and lenience to yourself from now on?

7.   Get perspective on failure

As a new leader, you will probably start off with a plan for everything to be perfect. By inviting the notion of becoming a bit more realistic and pragmatic, you can accept that failures are an essential part of growth and assist you in holding more realistic standards.

The next time you think you have failed, write down the potential outcomes of that failure and focus on accepting them. Once you have mentally reached a point where you can accept it, the fear loses its grip on you, and you can move forward more easily. More about this coming up.

8. Become more mindful

Do this by using the SBNRR technique we have already discussed or any other mindfulness techniques you may have learned before, like mindfulness meditation, taking up a yoga practice, or going for a meditative walk in nature. Take the time to be with yourself and clarify what is happening in your mind and body.

9. Have a feedback network and check in from time to time

It is great to have a person or people who can give you objective feedback so that you can evaluate what is real and where you have imposter distortions.

10. Don't fight your feelings

When you have challenging feelings, like feelings of not belonging, your natural tendency may be to shove them down and try your best to think positively. This is not a long-term solution; feelings want to be acknowledged; they are there to show us where things are not fine. Acknowledge your feelings and accept them, even make friends with them. This is how you will discover the core beliefs you have about yourself and your values, and it will empower you to begin unravelling these feelings.

11. Note your progress

Take accountability for your actions regularly. You can do this by keeping track of things you accomplish and how they impact you; remember to include both the positive and the negative.

12. Celebrate all your wins

Whether big or small, it will help you remain positive. How do you celebrate wins? You can start by writing them down in your "success journal", you can share them with people close to you, and you can even create a "Victory Ritual." At the end of every day, for example, you can allocate a few minutes to be alone, evaluate your victories for the day, and reward yourself by giving yourself a treat or just a big smile, focusing inwards, and thanking yourself for the things that you did well that day.

13. Get professional help

I have said this before, and I want to reiterate this point. Don't discount the pain you are going through and underestimate the importance of getting well. Take care of yourself by finding a professional if you are not managing well on your own.
One of the best solutions I have come across is to use an IS coach, someone who you can build a rapport with, who understands IS. If you have someone you are working with already, you may share resources like this book with them, to empower them to help you along your journey.

Sometimes having another person with a more subjective view of the situation, to guide and assist you can be the difference between breaking the cycle of imposter episodes or perpetuating your suffering.

14. Use Tools

Artificial intelligence is becoming a great part of our everyday lives. Make use of tools such as Risely, an AI-empowered leadership coaching platform to assist you.

Dealing with failure

Sometimes, we fail for real, and failure has consequences; we all know this already. For many of us, when we face the possibility of failing, our world crumbles, and the imposter inside of us comes to life once more.

What is failure?

Most people will agree that failure is when you set a goal and do not reach it. The trouble with this perspective is that failure can be very subjective, or as some say, "failure is in the eye of the beholder."

What if you do achieve your goal subjectively, but for some reason, it still feels and looks like a failure? This happened to me recently when I agreed to take on a project for a client and delivered high-quality work with an A+ effort, delivering what I believed to be precisely what the client had asked for. After delivering the project, I found out that the client felt dissatisfied because I did not spend enough time in the office (although I had no agreement with him to be office-bound). He subjectively valued facetime more than the successful completion of the deliverables.

Was I successful in my delivery? The answer is not a simple one. I went from a feeling of success after delivery to an immediate feeling of failure when I learned about the client's feelings.

How do you deal with this kind of ambiguity?

Reframe and recovering

Reframing failure involves changing your perspective on the situation to view it more positively. People do this all the time. Let's say you are an Olympic athlete, you have made it to the games, and instead of 1st place on the podium, you end up in third place.

Now, you can focus on your failure to be first, or you can acknowledge that most people will never even come close to qualifying, never mind taking 3rd place. The glass can indeed be either half full or half empty when it comes to the perception of success through different sets of eyes.

Of course, there is life after failing; it's all about how you react to what has happened.

How else can you define failure?

Change your perspective, and you can change your life. By casting a new light on a situation, you can move yourself from a feeling of failure to success. Here are some ways to do this:

- Take a beginner's mindset when you try something new, set a standard that is appropriate for a beginner. Allow yourself to be a novice.
- Allow yourself a learning curve. If you have had a failure, ask yourself if it could be that you are learning a new skill (highly commendable), take note of your lessons, and grow into an expert.
- Be aware of systemic bias and how that may make you feel like you have failed, even when, objectively, you've succeeded. There is a systemic bias against women, for example, the well-known gender pay gap, mentioned earlier. This fact may make you feel like you are failing because you earn less than your male counterparts. The trouble here is that you are fighting an age-old patriotically embedded tradition that does

not reflect your personal value or performance. Acknowledge that these biases exist and notice where they appear in your life.

- Cut yourself and others some slack. We live in a world full of ambiguity, and we are facing a highly volatile time; things are changing rapidly, and we are working hard to keep up with social, technological, and cultural changes. You are bound to make mistakes; we all are. Become honest about where you have failed due to lack of attention or care and where you did your best despite changing circumstances that challenged you to the point of perceived failure.
- Learn from failure and start to see it as part of the creative process; this way, you can keep your head straight and improve, or as some people call it, "fail upward." Like Thomas Edison, who famously found 10,000 ways that didn't work before he successfully invented the lightbulb. We can all benefit from being more like Thomas.
- Refocus and find new motivation. Realize that sometimes, a taste of failure is what you need to kick you out of complacency and comfort zones and inspire you to new heights of success.
- Often in life, things take time, and a failure can also be something that is not yet finished, or it may look like a failure, but it has served a purpose and can be filed as a win in a different category.

Distinguish mindfully: Success versus Failure

While failure is characterized by the failure to achieve a goal, success does not entail merely meeting a goal. It is bigger than that. While meeting a goal is an obvious and outward sign of success, you can also experience something called "process success," which is the success you achieve along the way. For example, if you decide to climb Mount

Kilimanjaro, reaching the summit is the "outcome success", but too often, we fail to recognize and appreciate the success you have along the way. The early morning training sessions, the discipline you maintained to keep a healthy diet leading up to your summit experience, and the mental preparation you did to make it all possible. If you can allow yourself to feel successful for the processes you go through and celebrate the small gains along the way, you will start cultivating a success feeling that will achieve a sense of overall success.

Understand the stages of failure

There are three stages of failure:

- Failure of vision, where you are not clear on what you want or your "why,"
- Failure of tactics, where you don't have a clear plan to get what you want, and
- Failure of strategy, where you know what you want, have a plan, follow the plan, and yet fail in the execution.

Simply understanding how failure works can help you increase your resilience in the face of failure. Failure, by the way, cannot be entirely avoided, but resilience is your crucial stepping stone to overcoming it. By practicing and maintaining the tips in this chapter, you will become more and more resilient. Eventually, you will no longer crumble but rather navigate a course when met with failure.

Don't fear failure

When you fear failure, you shy away from risks, stop excelling, and cease to grow. Stagnation is no way to live and will leave you feeling crippled, stuck, and unable to fulfil your full potential. Instead, keep working and building resilience, and you will become more brave and less afraid of failure.

Learn from failure

The most incredible learning curve in life is to turn a failure into a win. The only absolute failure is failing to learn from the lessons. How do you ensure you learn from your failures and avoid repeating them in the future?

Start by dissecting the failure at hand like a science project. Take a close look at it as a whole, do a root cause analysis, be honest with yourself, and get feedback. Ask yourself how it happened, where things went wrong, and what you could have done differently. Take note of your findings, internalize them, and you will be better equipped next time when faced with a similar situation.

Leading your team through their own IS

Seeing as a very large percentage of people will suffer from IS at some point in their lives, you will most certainly come across team members battling with this very same problem. Just like you, they will not be sure of what is going on or how to deal with it. Part of your role as a conscious leader is to guide and empower them to understand and overcome IS. This will be good for business, and it will make you feel successful when you see how your efforts are helping your team members overcome IS.

Unfortunately, IS thrives in workplaces with a dog-eat-dog culture, where competition and comparison are the order of the day, and where expectations are unclear, and communication is not a priority. When the workplace lacks diversity, this gets even worse.

Here's how you can become a pillar of support for your team in a toxic work environment:

Strengthen psychological safety

> **Psychological safety** is the belief that one will not be punished or humiliated for speaking up with ideas, questions, concerns, or mistakes.
> (Wikipedia
> https://en.wikipedia.org/wiki/Psychological_safety)

Promoting psychological safety in the workplace starts with having open discussions about IS and how self-doubt can accompany success. Have conversations with your team, tell them about IS, and share stories about how you have overcome it in your career, maybe even gift them a copy of this book, or place a copy in your office library.

It's important to normalize the fact that fear comes with taking risks and innovation. Let your team know it's okay to make mistakes and ask for help. Creating a container where IS is recognized and people know they are safe to share, even when they may feel intimidated, opens the flow of communication, and encourages your team to collaborate more freely, to define and solve problems more efficiently, creatively, and collaboratively. When you create this sense of safety, your team's well-being, and performance increase.

Today, I wish that my first managers had created this kind of safety for me. It would have saved me from many years of suffering in silence, made me a better worker, and helped me to deliver far better results in my early career.

Show what it means to work like a human

As a leader, it is important to understand that good mental and physical health is crucial to the team's performance.

If you want to...

(a) create long-term healthy relationships with your team members, and lifelong connections that will continue to serve you in your career or entrepreneurial path (today's interns are tomorrow's managers, the Vice President in 5 years, the President in 10, and the CEO, in 20 years),

(b) ensure that your team members are always at peak performance, and

(c) improve the human experience that you have at the workplace.

Then you should start by considering how you treat employees or team members. Do you acknowledge them as holistic beings, or are you only interested in their 'work face'?

If you want team members to feel valued as whole people with unique talents and goals, empathy is key. Ask yourself how you show understanding and validation, do you create a safe space where people can connect and thrive together? When a team member comes to you feeling overwhelmed and burnt out, and you notice signs of IS, are you willing to listen to them and share your struggles with the same feelings?

You can start shifting your approach today, and thereby help your teams. For example, build in breaks between meetings, encourage vacations, and delegate tasks instead of trying to do everything yourself. These small shifts will make a big difference. Your team will feel more supported and understood, and their performance will improve as a result.

Recognize people's accomplishments

The absolute best way I have found to boost my team's performance is to recognize and acknowledge the things that they do well, their special skill set, and then point out where they go the extra mile.

Once I had started praising people's efforts, instead of focusing on their outcomes, my team became more self-confident and more self-assured.

This alone is one of the most powerful changes you can make to not only help your team members (especially those who suffer from IS), but also to start to change the way that businesses treat their employees. Encouraging the "Whole Person" approach, instead of treating workers like machines, and expecting them to follow mechanical processes or instructions, opens our eyes to see them as creative individuals who can contribute more to the business as a whole.

Use feedback for development

One of your team members might be struggling with IS and feel that they're not good enough at their job, even though you think they have the adequate skills and experience to do it well. Using tools like 360 assessments and retrospectives is a method to help them combat these feelings, learn, and grow positively. When you give someone feedback, they understand what your expectations are, feel more confident in their abilities, and improve in the areas where they still need work to be done.

You can help them take an inventory of their strengths or put them in touch with a coach who can help them with this. A good coach helps discover the unique attributes that make you shine and supports consistent action to develop habits that propel your full potential (especially for people in underrepresented groups).

As Susan Tardanico put it, "It takes emotional honesty, introspection, and feedback from others to achieve the self-awareness and self-acceptance needed to combat Impostor Syndrome."

Encourage your team members to take time to reflect on their strengths and opportunities for growth, and to seek out the support they need to continue developing their skills and confidence. Remind them that they are capable and deserving of success!

Create a culture of inclusion

Imagine how much easier it would be to deal with IS in a workplace where there is space for honest conversations, without the fear of being seen as incompetent.

One way to ensure that you create a climate of inclusion is to allow team members to speak without interruption and to listen intently so that you can understand their questions, and concerns, or opinions. When people feel heard, they feel valued, and when team members feel valued, they will not only be more productive, but they will also come to trust you and become more loyal to you.

As we close the chapter focusing on the range of tools available to fight IS, I will leave you with some tips on how to deal with each of the different imposter types that we discovered in chapter 3. These can be tried on yourself, and team members, alike.

Tools for each Imposter Type

Imposter Syndrome is not something that you should leave alone to 'heal by itself', it won't just disappear, and the effects on your life and career will be over-whelming if you do not deal with it. Over time it will eat away at your confidence and self-worth and contribute a generous portion to decreased job performance and satisfaction.

Just knowing that you have it is not enough; you will need to take firm action to regain control. This section groups together the strategies to beat the seven types of Imposter Syndrome we discussed in Chapter 3.

Tools for The Perfectionist

- Go for GEQ - Good Enough Quality. As I mentioned earlier, every project does not have to be perfect, you don't have to be perfect. You can break the cycle of over-preparing by taking action. Get started, take that first step, and submit that first draft. I repeat, it does not have to be perfect. (That goes for any typos you find in this book too!).
- Affirm to yourself that 75% is good enough.
- Learn to accept unfinished work: Grab a pen and paper and draw for 2 minutes with a particular idea in mind, such as a pet or your car. Try to add as much detail as possible, but don't rush. When the timer ends, examine your drawing. Don't worry if it's incomplete; the goal of this exercise is to accept unfinished work.
- Check your goals again. Are they realistic? Have you set realistic deadlines and targets?

Tools for the Superhero

- Set boundaries for yourself when it comes to performance-driven activities like work. Remind yourself that your worth is not equal to your outputs and that you are enough, without having to do anything and limit the time you spend on production-foouood activitioc.
- Celebrate your achievements. While it is natural for you to want to move on to the next victory

immediately, take the time to revel in the fruits of your labour and acknowledge your success.

- Delegate and collaborate, force yourself to let go of that "I can do it all" attitude and allow those around you to help you, thereby also empowering them to shine.
- Discover your own passions and figure out what really lights you up. This can be a game-changer in creating a well-rounded sense of self, outside of your job.

Tools for The Natural Genius

- Cultivate a growth mindset and begin to view yourself as a "work in progress." Know that you can improve yourself and squash the belief that you are stuck with the skills you were born with. This will empower you to put in the effort you need to get better when you lack skills or abilities.
- Encourage yourself to attempt skills that you are not proficient in rather than categorizing them as something you are incapable of doing.
- Ask for advice from people who excel in their fields and ask about their initial difficulties and how they got better.
- Understand that everyone must start somewhere and that the process of becoming competent is just as deserving of admiration as the final outcome.
- Avoid labelling tasks as things you "can't do" and connect with experts to learn about their early struggles. This will help you realize that everyone starts somewhere on their journey.

Tools for The Rugged Individualist

- Surround yourself with the right people, spend time with dream creators, and avoid the naysayers of big dreams.

- Once you have the right people, learn how to brief, and manage them properly to maximize your chances of a successful collaboration.
- Consider joining a mastermind program to connect with highly skilled people who empower you.
- Chat with someone you respect and ask them how other people have played a role in their success. It's a great way to get a fresh perspective.

Tools for The Expert

- Mentor some of your junior colleagues or sign up to volunteer. Doing this is an excellent way to discover your own expertise and help you feel less like a fraud.
- Embrace the idea of being a lifelong student and accept that knowledge is unlimited, and you will never know everything as you continue to grow and learn throughout your life.
- Discipline yourself to only learn new skills when you need them instead of compulsively over-preparing. In this way, you will excel at specific things you need to excel in instead of trying to learn everything and perhaps absorbing less.
- Set reasonable and healthy expectations for yourself, it is not reasonable to expect anyone else to know everything on any given subject, so why is it reasonable to expect that of yourself? Keep telling yourself that you will have the ability to learn what you need to when you need it, and that is good enough.
- Ask for feedback, your colleagues and friends will be able to point out to you if there are any areas that you lack knowledge or skills that are important. This way, you can focus your attention on the areas that need work, without having to compulsively collect new information.

Tools for the Noticer

- Accept yourself. People pleasing causes you to lose touch with yourself and allows others' opinions of you to determine your value. Accept your imperfections, and your humanness and move forward. When you do this, other people will follow suit and accept you in return.
- Stop dwelling on past mistakes. Let go of things that weigh you down, cut out toxic people, and take actions that will make you happy.
- Stop comparing yourself to others. This is non-negotiable if you want to overcome this type of IS. Accept that every person has their own journey and that comparing your internal world to the external world of another person will only lead to a feeling of despondence and anxiety.
- Focus on creating support systems around you and on building relationships with people that will help you feel a sense of belonging. This will help you feel more secure in your connections and less critical of your performance.

Tools for the Discounter

- Keep a success file, as we looked at earlier in this chapter. This will help to remind you of your successes as you go.
- Ask for validation. When you have done something well, and you hear yourself discounting your success, deliberately ask for feedback so that you can use that external validation to remind yourself that your success is real.
- Like the Noticer type, you will also benefit from building and strengthening your support systems. When you have closer trusting relationships with others, you will be more likely to take their word for it when they tell you that you are doing well.

- Take stock of your abilities regularly. Being honest with yourself about what you are good at, and where you need work will help you stay in touch with the truth about your success and will help keep you from the trap of discounting your achievements.

Bringing it all together

I would like to encourage you to read this chapter again and make a habit of working through the tools every so often. This will be a constant reminder of how you can take control to feel better and become more resilient with time.

In this chapter, we have looked at some of the immediate things you can do in your battle against IS, these tools work well in case-to-case scenarios. If, however, you're looking for something more long-term, you'll have to start working on yourself on a deeper level. Are you ready to conquer your IS for good? Then let's keep going…

Chapter 5 - Becoming Self-Made

"Ofttimes nothing profits more than self-esteem, grounded on just and right well managed."

- John Milton,
Paradise Lost,
Book VIII, line 571

Become the CEO of your life

The best way to fully recover from and avoid Imposter Syndrome, with the longest-lasting effects, is to become the best version of yourself and to do that, you need to take care of yourself in the best possible way.

Most of us lead our lives never really looking out for or loving ourselves, giving too much, being hard on ourselves for our imperfections, and always trying to be more, do more, and give more.

When I was younger, I would often over-give to my partners and, eventually, my spouse and my bosses because I assumed that they would look out for me as long as I kept giving. Life, however, has taught me that if I want to have the experiences I want, I must take responsibility for leading myself toward them. One day I came across the idea of appointing myself as the CEO of my life. I created the habit of conversing with myself every day before the day started and officially setting myself as the Chief Executive Officer of the venture that is my life.

How would your life be different if, tomorrow, you appointed yourself as the CEO of your life?

What does it even mean to be the CEO of your life? Let's look at the role description of a CEO. According to Investopedia, the CEO of an enterprise is responsible for "making major corporate decisions, managing overall operations, and setting the company's strategic direction."

Translated into Life-CEO, it can be rewritten as:

The CEO of your life is responsible for making major life decisions, managing overall behaviour, and determining the life experiences you want.

Now ask yourself,

- When you make major decisions in your life, how much attention do you pay to your own needs, and how deliberate are you about making great quality decisions that will benefit you and lead you towards the experiences you want?
- How do you manage your behaviour, and how well does that serve you in every area of your life? How does your behaviour help you get closer to the life experiences that you want?
- What are the experiences that you want in your life? Do you know what you value?

For me, being the CEO of my life means leading myself. Charles Manz coined the term 'self-leadership', defining it as "a comprehensive self-influence perspective that concerns leading oneself."

What does a "comprehensive self-influence perspective" mean? To me, it means that I know myself, I understand myself (an ongoing process of course), and because I know and understand myself, I know what I want to experience in life.

What does leading yourself mean? It means that you direct your energy, the actions that you take, towards things that will bring you closer to your goals (the experiences you want in life).

Leading your life goes beyond management, beyond daily tasks and lists and getting things done; it is about having a higher awareness of yourself and taking strategic action towards your desired future. To really lead your life like a seasoned CEO, you first must know which experiences you want in your future.

Lead Yourself

Self-leadership is about taking charge of your own actions and motivation. It involves setting goals, being proactive, and managing yourself effectively to achieve success. By developing self-awareness, utilizing self-motivation techniques, and practicing self-discipline, you can become an effective leader in your own life.

Self-leadership is not only about doing the things that come naturally; it is also about leading yourself toward doing the things that *do not* come naturally therefore, self-control, which includes self-regulation and self-management, are all crucial aspects of self-leadership. It is about taking conscious steps to bridge the gap between where you are today and where you want to be.

Sometimes you will feel the internal drive to do something (intrinsic motivation), and sometimes you will feel external pressure to get something done while you do not feel self-motivated to do it; as you lead yourself well, you will learn to regulate and manage yourself so that you will be able to lead yourself successfully in both instances.

Self-control becomes much easier when your goals are aligned with your purpose, as more of your actions will become internally driven. Even when you have to do something that does not feel aligned at the moment, you will still be able to lead yourself through it and towards your goals using self-control because the outcome is aligned with your values. There is a direct link between motivation, purpose, and focus, and it is important to be internally regulated and intrinsically motivated if you want to live a truly successful life.

When you can harmonize your thoughts, emotions, and actions, you create a powerful synergy that propels you forward. However, it is the driving force of **purpose** that truly guides you in the right direction. Purpose serves as a compass, providing clarity and meaning to our endeavours. It aligns your actions with your core values and aspirations.

Self-leadership as a form of self-care

You must become certain of what you want, and you can then develop habits, routines, and rituals that help you self-regulate. You need discipline to stay on track. This is what self-care is truly about. It is not about luxury bubble baths and spa days (although they *are* needed every now and then!).

I would like to mention that self-care and self-development go together. When you care for yourself, you will develop yourself. But again, what does self-development mean?

Self-development refers to the intentional and continuous process of improving yourself in various aspects of life, including personal growth, skills enhancement, and mindset development. It involves acquiring new knowledge, honing existing skills, and cultivating positive habits to become a better version of yourself.

To develop yourself, you need to circle back to your values, then your goals, and the skills and tools you need to become more efficient at doing the things that are required to reach your goals. You need to value yourself enough, love yourself enough, respect your time, and be willing to set boundaries, make sacrifices and do what you need to do to become the best version of yourself, to develop yourself into the person that you need to be to attain your most ambitious goals. In that way, you will come closer and closer to self-actualization.

As a very simple example, I have a goal to eat only organic, non-GMO food. Which requires me to cook from scratch – with raw wholefoods; no packet sauces, no "cheat" products full of synthetic preservatives, emulsifiers, and stabilisers.
This goal, whilst great for my health, is not great for my bank balance. It is also time-consuming, it requires more meal prep, better cooking skills and the inconvenience of having to visit several different stores for ingredients. However, because it is a goal I value highly, I find the discipline, I make the time, I learn to follow more complicated recipes and as a result I have now formed habits that make the process enjoyable. I also spend more time outdoors tending my vegetable and herb garden!

Know Yourself

When you know yourself (let's call it having more self-awareness), you can better regulate yourself, better prepare and reduce wasted time and energy. How so? Well, let's look at these simple examples;

Knowing your personality traits can help you predict your thoughts, feelings, and behaviours. With this knowledge at your fingertips, you can act more strategically in everything you do. For example, the personality trait of conscientiousness is a good indicator of your ability to self-lead. Conversely, if you are not so conscientious, you can achieve quick wins by developing a laser focus on improving this one aspect of yourself.

Being aware of your personal strengths and weaknesses can help you understand why you procrastinate with some things and do others without hesitation. When you know this, you can find ways to link the things you procrastinate over to your values to find motivation, you can also sharpen any skills you lack and improve motivation in that way, or you can choose to say no to things that you know do not serve you and that you have no real interest in.

I, for example am a self-confessed "control freak". I procrastinate over delegation. But I value teamwork and I know that team work ultimately makes for a more successful outcome. Therefore, I plan in extra time to specify exactly what I want from my team in a work brief, as well as extra time to review their work once it's complete. With proper templates in place to ensure I don't miss anything, I am much more motivated to delegate work.

Knowing your values will help you understand the choices you make and will also help you make high-quality decisions for your life and future. It will help you set SMART goals, as we will see later, and help you find internal motivation.

For example, I know I value free time, so mastering delegation and using software tools for efficiency come high up on my list of priorities.

Understanding your talents and interests empowers you to put your strengths to work in an enjoyable way, while also maximizing your likelihood of success.

I love editing imagery in Photoshop or designing in Canva, so these aspects of my job I like to keep to myself, for other tasks I delegate, because I understand that it is quicker and more efficient for others who love those tasks to do them than me. Otherwise, I know I will end up procrastinating and avoiding the tasks I don't like, meaning they take much longer to get completed, (if they get done at all!).

Find out what you want

As humans, we thrive on goals, and we feel happier when we reach our goals. Sounds quite simple, right? But then, why are we not happier if it is that simple? It turns out that we are not that good at knowing what we want. Often, we end up setting goals for ourselves that are not truly aligned with our values, and naturally, we don't enjoy the process of reaching our goals as much. Likewise, when we do reach these goals, we don't feel much happiness because we were aiming for something we didn't really want in the first place.

When you think of it this way, it is easy to see why you may be living in perpetual dissatisfaction. To solve this conundrum, it is crucial to become aware of your values and have a clear understanding of what you want in your life and what kind of things and experiences you wish to have.

This brings us right back to self-reflection. To really know what you want, you must reflect on your own values and take the time and energy to get to the bottom of what makes you tick.

Then set SMART goals

When you hear someone talk about goal setting, your first thought may be that it does not apply to you because you may already know where you are headed; you may have already done a goal-setting exercise at some point in your life. What you may not realize is that your goals may shift over time, and as you come closer to understanding yourself, you may want to reevaluate your goals.

The thing is that once you have taken the time to understand your values as they are today, and once you truly know what experiences you want at the moment (as opposed to what you thought you wanted 1, 2, 3, or even ten years ago), you can set new goals or update your existing goals to be closely aligned with your values. The next step is then to make sure your goals are crystal clear so that you can break them down into smaller goals and more manageable milestones that are clearly defined.

To do this, you can use the SMART goals method which we will go into in more detail in chapter 8, but for now, here is a quick introduction.

Every goal you set should be:

Specific: Instead of saying, "I want to exercise more," make it specific by stating, "I will go for a 30-minute walk every morning before work."

Measurable: If your goal is to drink more water, set a measurable target of drinking eight glasses of water each day and track your daily intake.

Achievable: If you want to improve your fitness level, start with smaller milestones, like being able to run a 5K race in three months if you're currently a beginner.

Relevant: If your goal is to improve your career prospects, focus on developing a new skill or completing a certification that is relevant to your desired career path.

Time-bound: Instead of saying, "I will read more books," set a time-bound goal like, "I will read two books per month for the next six months" to give yourself a clear timeframe.

Once you have set SMART goals for yourself, you want to give yourself the best chance to reach these goals. That means figuring out what's holding you back.

The way you think and manage your thoughts has a profound impact on your likelihood of achieving your goals, as well as the time it will take you to reach them. Your mind can be your greatest weapon in the journey to achieving your goals, but it can also be your greatest enemy when you do not control it properly.

Have you ever had an experience where you wake up in the morning, you have a list of things to do to make your life work and to get closer to your goals, and you are ready to take on the day. But then something happens to derail you. It can be an upsetting phone call, an encounter with a rude cashier, a child throwing a tantrum, a particular look from your partner, or a comment from your boss or a client, and next thing you know, your mind takes you into a downward spiral of self-doubt, anger, fear, sadness, guilt, or all of these at once.

Now you are barely able to get through the day without losing your cool; all hope of a productive, happy day is out the window, as the battlefield in your mind keeps you going through a loop, and your internal dialogue takes a turn for the worst: *"What else can go wrong?"*, *"What could I have said to that person?"*, *"Why is this happening to me?"*, *"I am a bad person?"*, *"I can't do this,"* *"I am a mess,"* *"Everything is falling apart."*...does this sound familiar at all?

If it does, the good news is that, again, you are not alone. This type of thinking is not a character flaw, but instead, it is a very natural reaction to life events, especially when you have an untrained mind. Even better news is that you can train your mind to take you into upward spirals or at least remain stable, even when facing challenges.

Let's take a closer look at some reasons why your mind tends to take you on these wild journeys.

Hardwired Responses

The fight-or-flight response is primal and deeply ingrained within us all. It is a survival mechanism finely tuned by millions of years of evolution. When faced with a perceived threat, whether physical or emotional, your body instinctively responds with a surge of energy, preparing you to either stand your ground and confront the danger or flee from it. This remarkable response is hardwired into your biology and was responsible for our ancestors' survival in the face of perilous situations.

Think back to a time when you felt your heart race, your muscles tense, and your senses sharpened - all in an instant. That was your fight-or-flight response in action. It's a natural, automatic process that occurs within milliseconds; it gets triggered by the brain's alarm system, the amygdala. When it senses danger, it sends signals to various parts of your body, activating the release of stress hormones like adrenaline and cortisol, propelling you into a heightened state of readiness. You will either run away, fight back, or freeze in the face of danger.

Understanding this response is crucial because it explains why you might experience overwhelming emotions, such as fear, anxiety, or anger, in certain situations. By acknowledging the primal origins of these intense reactions, you can begin to take control of your response and harness its power to navigate.

Understand cognitive dissonance

Next, let's delve into the intriguing concept of cognitive dissonance, a phenomenon that causes internal conflict when your beliefs and actions clash. It's that uneasy feeling you get when your thoughts, values, or beliefs are at odds with your actions or outside reality.

For example, imagine you are a manager who highly values fairness and inclusivity, yet you consistently favour one team member over another. This behaviour creates a noticeable discrepancy between your belief in fairness and your actions (favouring one team member). This can cause cognitive dissonance, an uncomfortable recognition of inconsistency within yourself. This internal conflict can be disconcerting, leaving you in a state of unease or turmoil.

To resolve this dissonance, you will most likely find yourself rationalizing your actions by convincing yourself that the favoured team member has superior skills or deserves special treatment. By creating justifications that align with your actions, you will attempt to reduce the dissonance and restore inner harmony.

Start Acting - you can do this!

If you are anything like me, it is not easy to acknowledge that you are ruled by the fight-or-flight response, and even less easy to admit that cognitive dissonance is a part of your make-up. We all like to believe that we are fair and just and act rationally at all times.

That's okay, take a moment to accept that these behaviours are hard-wired, and they are the default reactions of all human beings. And then, you can come to the empowering understanding that you can conquer these limiting behaviours and reactions. By consciously working on yourself to make decisions rationally and tapping into your full potential to do so, you can become better at managing yourself.

The first steps, knowing yourself, creating intrinsic motivation, and setting SMART goals, we have already looked at; now let's look at some more insights that may help you and the daily actions you can take to lead yourself to optimal success.

Real life inspiration to prove that this stuff works

Victor Frankl, an Austrian psychiatrist, and Holocaust survivor is an excellent example of how various aspects of self-leadership can play a crucial role, even in survival. Let's look at his behaviour during his time in the concentration camps, and how the traits we touched on above, served him in that trying time.

Self-awareness: Frankl showed self-awareness by recognizing and acknowledging his emotions, thoughts, and reactions to the extreme circumstances he faced. This self-awareness allowed him to maintain a sense of control over his inner world, even when his external circumstances were completely beyond his control.

Purpose and meaning: His concept of logotherapy emphasizes the importance of finding meaning in life, even in the face of immense suffering. During his time in the camp, he held onto the belief that his existence had a purpose, which gave him the will to endure and persevere.

Self-regulation and resilience: Frankl exhibited tremendous self-regulation by not only acknowledging but also managing his emotions, thoughts, and behaviours during unimaginable hardship. He chose how to respond to his circumstances, focusing on maintaining his dignity and kindness towards others and holding on to hope.

Positive mindset: Frankl maintained a positive mindset; he believed in the power of finding meaning and purpose in even the most difficult situations, which helped him maintain hope and optimism.

Self-compassion and empathy: Frankl extended compassion not only to others but also to himself. He showed understanding and kindness towards his suffering, acknowledging his vulnerability while at the same time striving to support and uplift others.

Goal setting and action: Throughout his time in the concentration camp, Frankl set meaningful goals for himself, such as completing his manuscript on logotherapy. These goals gave him a sense of direction and purpose, allowing him to maintain control.

Putting the 'self' in yourself

We've talked about self-leadership, and we've talked about the mental aspects of self-care, but what about self-love? Throughout my life, I have heard from different people that self-love is essential, yet I never really understood what self-love meant. How do you learn to love yourself if it does not come naturally? Is it something that can be learned, and is it possible to consistently love yourself, even when you seem unlovable in your actions and behaviour?

For me, self-love is about respecting myself and knowing my value. When I appreciate myself enough that I naturally do things that support my spiritual growth as well as my physical and psychological well-being. Self-love is essential for a thriving life, and when I learned to love myself, my world changed. I went from living with a sense of constant persecution to living a peaceful life free of internal negative self-talk.

What exactly is self-compassion?

Self-compassion, in a nutshell, is about being kind and understanding to yourself when you fail. We were asked during a training session once to write a letter to someone we love in which we addressed a personal failure of that person. Once we'd finished the letter, and after we talked about self-love and self-compassion, we were then asked to think of a recent failure we'd had. Then, you guessed it, we were asked to rewrite the letter, but this time, write the letter to ourselves, showing the same understanding and compassion that we had in the letter to a loved one. It was astonishing to see how much kinder we were to our loved ones than we were to ourselves.

Kristin Neff, an expert in self-compassion, defines it as the ability to notice our suffering and to be moved by it, making you want to do something to actively reduce your suffering.

Self-compassion, according to Neff, is made up of three components:

1. **Self-kindness instead of self-judgment:**
   Instead of criticizing yourself for making a mistake, you can practice self-kindness by offering understanding and support to yourself. For example, if you fail at a task, you might say, "It's okay to make mistakes. Everyone has setbacks. I will learn from this experience and be kind to myself."

2. **Common humanity instead of isolation:**
   Instead of feeling alone in your struggles, you can recognize that everyone faces challenges and experiences imperfection. You can acknowledge that it's a normal part of being human. For instance, if I feel inadequate in a social situation, I remind myself, "Others may also feel nervous or insecure. We are all navigating similar emotions and situations."

3. **Mindfulness instead of over-identification:**
    Instead of getting caught up in your thoughts and
    emotions, you can practice mindfulness by looking at your
    thoughts without judgment. For example, if you're angry
    or sad, allow yourself to fully experience and acknowledge
    those emotions without getting carried away. You might
    say, "I notice that I'm feeling angry right now. It's okay to
    feel this way, and I will observe it with compassion and let
    it pass."

Common misconceptions about self-compassion

You, like many other people, may think that you should be
careful of placing too much emphasis on yourself and that it is
more virtuous to focus on others and give more than you
receive. It is almost seen as a sin to give to yourself. This kind
of thinking, unfortunately, creates the risk of depriving you of
using tools like self-compassion, that can help you feel better
and be more successful. Let's look at the most common
misconceptions people fall into that make us dismiss self-
compassion as a way to feel better:

Myth 1: Self-compassion is the same as self-pity.

Self-compassion is not about wallowing in our feelings forever.
Research shows that self-compassionate people ruminate
less and experience fewer symptoms of anxiety and
depression.

Myth 2: Self-compassion is self-excuse.

Self-compassionate people, in fact, are more motivated to
apologize when they have caused harm and are committed to
not repeating their behaviour. Self-compassion strengthens
your personal accountability, providing a heightened sense of
responsibility.

Myth 3: Self-compassion is self-serving.

Contrary to the belief that self-compassion is selfish, research shows that self-compassionate people have better relationships. They are more caring, affectionate, considerate, and accepting of imperfections.

Myth 4: Self-compassion equals self-esteem.

While self-esteem is often tied to success or failure, self-compassion gives you emotional resilience, and helps you make better decisions, it prevents you from overestimating yourself and making reckless choices.

Myth 5: Self-compassion is de-motivating.

Self-compassionate people understand the importance of sustained effort and long-term success. By acknowledging your current position and your limitations, you can pace yourself for long-term performance and remove the expectations of immediate payoff that you may be harbouring.

By actively rejecting and dispelling these misconceptions, you can embrace self-compassion as a powerful tool for personal growth, well-being, and meaningful relationships.

How can you start practicing self-compassion?

The journey of cultivating self-compassion can be a challenging one, especially in a world that constantly demands more from us and reinforces feelings of inadequacy. This is especially true for those of us who have faced obstacles and barriers in our life. The crucial first step you can take is to recognize this fact.

By acknowledging the complexity of our world and struggles, we can build deeper compassion, not only for ourselves but also for others.

Once you have decided to live a life of self-compassion and you have shifted your mindset to this new way of being, there are some specific things you can do, practices if you will, to help you increase your self-compassion every day:

Physical touch: Increase self-compassion in your daily life by engaging in simple physical gestures like placing a hand on your forearm or your heart, then applying gentle pressure to activate your internal care system. Add to this a self-compassionate affirmation to acknowledge your struggles and shared human experiences.

Enhance emotional agility: Recognize and understand your feelings and needs by spending time with yourself and journaling about how you feel and what you need. Doing this will also increase your empathy and compassion for other people.

Practice mindfulness: Mindfulness meditation can help you observe and nurture self-compassion. Recognize what is happening, allow the experience to be present, investigate it with care, and nurture yourself with mindful self-compassion. There are many guided meditation recordings on YouTube and Spotify; these are great resources for practicing mindfulness.

Externalize your inner critic: Visualize your inner critic as a separate entity, give it a name, and maybe even a cartoon character-like appearance. Doing this will help you regain a sense of control and recognize its intentions while reframing its messages as motivators rather than absolute truths about yourself.

Doing these exercises and techniques regularly develops a stronger foundation of self-compassion and brings more kindness and understanding into your life. You will be challenged along the way of course, especially if you have perfectionistic tendencies like me.

The Psychology of Self-Love and Self-Compassion

When you practice self-compassion, you can be honest with yourself, admit your limitations and flaws, and look at yourself objectively. This differs somewhat from self-esteem, which is based on your sense of self-worth or how much you value yourself. Self-compassion is not based on self-evaluation; it is available to everyone, regardless of your perceived value of yourself or accomplishments. You deserve self-compassion simply for the mere fact that you are human.

What about self-confidence and self-compassion? How are they related? Again, self-confidence is about feeling good about your abilities and the perceived value of your abilities, while self-compassion does not rely on your abilities. You can, when you are compassionate with yourself, admit where you are limited, and you can still be kind to yourself.

When you look at these concepts with a sense of self-awareness and introspection, you may wonder where the line between healthy self-love and narcissism lies. Firstly, self-love is not about comparing yourself to others but about being proud of your accomplishments and validating yourself, while narcissism, in my experience, is all about comparing yourself to others, looking the part, needing validation from others, and being inflexible.

The difference is in the honesty and authenticity with which you look at yourself instead of focusing on how others see you, which is the basis of narcissistic behaviour.

An example of healthy self-love and self-compassion

Julia had always been a high achiever throughout her life. She excelled in sports and academics and breezed through college, finding it easy to balance academics and a thriving social life. When she entered the workplace, she got her dream job in no time at all, and she quickly started climbing the corporate ladder.

From the outside, her life looked perfect, and she was one of those people whom others would envy because she just seemed to have it all together.

She married the man of her dreams, and together they built a thriving life together.

Inside herself, she had started to take strain, however. While academics came easy to her, real-life work situations were a different story. She found it hard to make boundaries and say "No," and she constantly felt like an imposter in the male-dominated industry she worked in.

She was forever on a quest to become better at her job, to do more at home, and to be more supportive of the people in her life.

Until, at some point, things started to change; she woke up one morning and realized that something was not right, and it hadn't been right for a while. She was feeling down all the time, she had no energy, and she felt like she could not keep up with the demands of her life any longer. She tried to get better; she knew many people needed her at peak performance, and she did not have the luxury of taking time off or being unwell.

Then she hit rock bottom; it happened suddenly and unexpectedly. In her worn-out state, while trying to still be the superwoman she always was, she made an error at work, one that cost the company one of its biggest clients. At the same time, she discovered that her husband had been unfaithful to her, and she felt like her life was crumbling around her.

Seeing the signs of distress in Julia's life, a close friend recommended a therapist to her and motivated her to seek out counselling. By now, Julia had fallen into some unhealthy habits to deal with the pain, and she was spiralling into a downward pattern of self-destructive behaviour.

After several sessions of trauma healing Julia managed to regain her drive to live a meaningful life and rebuild what had been lost. The first step, she discovered, was to learn to love herself.

She started to reframe what had happened in her career. Instead of continuing to scold herself and continuing to dwell on the mistake she made, she decided to practice self-compassion. She started to acknowledge to herself that mistakes happen to everyone and that she deserves to be treated with kindness and understanding. She reframed the situation as a learning opportunity and then focused on creating systems in her work to prevent similar mistakes in the future. She also created a daily habit of affirming words of encouragement to herself and reminding herself that a single error, even if it had devastating effects, does not define her worth.

Despite her busy schedule, she prioritized self-care, setting aside time for activities that bring her joy and recharge her energy. She realized that investing in her happiness benefits not only herself but also her relationships and her overall quality of life. Today, she consistently carves out time for self-love, she takes moments of solitude to reflect and process her emotions, and she nurtures her mental, emotional, and physical well-being, allowing her to show up as the best version of herself in all areas of her life.

Julia also actively and intentionally practices tolerance and patience with herself; she does not allow her inner critic to say mean things to her, and she acknowledges that personal growth is a journey that takes time, reminding herself that it's okay to have flaws and areas for improvement, as they are part of being human. Every day, she takes small steps, celebrates progress, and extends the same understanding and acceptance she offers others toward herself.

Whenever she feels unworthy or 'less than,' she reminds herself that feelings of inadequacy are not unique to her; many people share them. Rather than internalizing these feelings as a personal failure, she recognizes them as a shared human experience. She understands that everyone has moments of self-doubt and insecurities, even those who may appear confident on the surface.

Day-to-day she chooses to focus on her strengths, accomplishments, and the progress she has made. She actively seeks opportunities for personal growth and learning, knowing that these experiences contribute to her overall development.

It has been 12 months since she got help, and her life today is unrecognizable. She has gained a healthy amount of self-love, and she manages her life and responsibilities with grace and a peaceful competence that comes from being true to her own values. Recognizing that self-love and self-compassion are lifelong journeys; she gets back on track with her self-care habits whenever she notices that life is pulling her in other directions. She knows that life will improve with each passing day if she just takes care of the basics.

Benefits of learning to love yourself

You will feel better - Your self-esteem and self-worth increase as you accept yourself. When there is no longer a war going on inside you, everything feels better. Your mindset changes, you become more resilient, and you feel less stressed. Mental health issues, like depression and anxiety, improve and can disappear entirely.

Your relationships become healthier - Loving yourself is the critical foundation to healthy, functional relationships with others. When you love yourself, you can set healthy boundaries and communicate better, and your relationships are based on mutual support and respect.

You grow - When you love yourself and are compassionate toward yourself, you are more likely to chase your goals, take risks, and do things that fulfil you.

You become more authentic and empowered - you learn to live by your values and what you want. You stop seeking validation from others, instead making decisions aligned with your true self, and your life becomes more fulfilling.

You become resilient - you bounce back from setbacks quickly, with kindness and understanding.

How to practice self-love (and acceptance)

As I have mentioned, learning to love yourself is a lifetime journey. As you grow and change, you'll discover parts of yourself that will challenge your ability to love yourself, but every day of loving yourself is a gift and a miracle, especially if you come from a place where you don't love yourself much. The first step towards self-love is establishing where you stand in your relationship with yourself.

To help with that, you can take the Neffs self-compassion test[1] by pointing your phone camera at this QR code and following the link.

Set some time aside, about 15 minutes, and get into a reflective state (with no outside disturbances) so that you can take an honest stock of where you are today and start working towards a more loving relationship with yourself.

---

[1] https://self-compassion.org/self-compassion-test/

Let's recap

Up to this point, we've looked at the essence of leadership, and what the difference is between management and leadership.

In Chapter 2, we took a deep dive into the common leadership challenges you will likely face.

Then in Chapter 3, we introduced the biggest challenge of them all, Imposter Syndrome. We took a close look at how and why we see this so frequently. We went as far as identifying different types of imposters along with tools to identify your unique flavour of IS;

- the Perfectionist
- the Natural Genius
- the Rugged Individualist
- the Expert
- the Noticer
- the Discounter
- the Superwoman

In Chapter 4, we took the first step towards overcoming IS, giving you some easy-to-use, practical tools to get you started on your journey straight away.

In this chapter, we looked at how you can use self-love and self-care as a longer-term solution to your battle with IS.

Self-care and self-development both go hand in hand. But how do you get started with the latter?

Coach, co-ordinator, supervisor, team captain, manager, or any role – whether personal or professional – that puts you in a leadership position requires a certain set of skills.

These skills, when studied and put into practice, can be a game-changer, especially when you master them early on!

Spread across the next 6 chapters, we will look at each of these 15 critical leadership skills.

Self-Development Skills
1. Empathy
2. Emotional Intelligence

Strategic Skills
3. Strategic Thinking
4. Creating and Communicating a Vision

Planning & Action Skills
5. Goal Setting
6. Decision-making
7. Problem-solving

Communication Skills
8. Active Listening
9. Effective Communication
10. Building Rapport

People Management Skills
11. Encouraging and Motivating Others
12. Giving and Receiving Feedback
13. Delegation

Team Management Skills
14. Autonomy and Accountability
15. Collaboration and Conflict Resolution

As well as these 15 skills, we will take a deep dive into the number one mistake many new leaders make, and the devastating effects it always has on teams and businesses.

Part II

Chapter 6 - Grow Like a Leader

*"Wouldn't it be wonderful if we could all
be a little more gentle with each other,
and a little more loving, have a little more
empathy, and maybe we'd like each other
a little bit more."*

- Judy Garland,
As quoted in Little Girl Lost (1974)

Early in my career, I had a mentor who changed the course of my life, by introducing me to **Empathy** and **Emotional Intelligence**, the first two skills we will look at.

I remember him fondly as the kindest and most caring person I ever worked for. He demanded absolute honesty and ethical behaviour from his team and in return he created an atmosphere that I can only describe as the ideal work environment a leader can strive for.

At the time I did not understand why he was so different from the other leaders I worked for, but today I understand that the difference in him was that he had high levels of both empathy and emotional intelligence.

Empathy

What is Empathy?

Empathy, often defined as "walking a mile in another's shoes," is the number one way to build understanding and authentic bonds between people.

Defined as having the ability to experience and share others' emotions. The term empathy was first coined in 1908, borrowing from the German philosopher Rudolf Lotze's (1817-1881) phrase "Einfuhlung," first used to translate the Greek term "empatheia," meaning passion and emotion, to English.

Empathy, unfortunately, isn't universal - some people are naturally empathetic, while others must consciously work to develop empathy. Interestingly, having a higher socioeconomic status may reduce your empathy levels. If you find it very easy to pick up on others' emotions and you have deep compassion for their struggles without even being told about it directly, congratulations, you are probably more empathetic than most. While you may have cursed your empathetic nature in the past, and you may have even been labelled as overly sensitive, your empathy can become your superpower. You see, empathy allows you to connect on a fundamental level so that you can build trusting relationships and create a sense of belonging. In leadership situations, it allows you to guide and support team members more effectively so they can flourish into being their best selves.

Why is Empathy so Valuable?

When you have higher empathy levels, you tend to help others, even when doing so goes against your self-interest, and in a group when empathy is valued and promoted, the entire group may start showing more altruistic behaviours - making working together in harmony much easier. At the same time, empathy combats prejudice, racism and even bullying. It also motivates us to help those outside our social circles - including stigmatized people like the poor or disabled.

The benefits of empathy in the workplace are clear; leaders who show more empathetic behaviour see employees who miss less work due to sickness and report higher happiness levels.

A Word of Warning

At this point, I should warn you about the link between empathy and stress. When you empathize with someone, you tap into their emotions and experience a physiological reaction within yourself - you actually feel them! Therefore, becoming more empathetic may expose you to other people's stresses and struggles, which can both benefit you and challenge you at the same time.

Imagine being the leader of a high-pressure work environment, and one of your team members is experiencing personal troubles. When you are highly empathetic, you will feel their discomfort and emotional turmoil. While this will help you to connect more deeply, it also adds another level of stress for you. Suddenly, you may find yourself shouldering their burden and feel responsible for making them feel better or for fixing their problems. When left unchecked, this tendency to want to rescue can lead to emotional exhaustion and burnout when you internalize the stresses of others.

As you learn how to grow your empathy, also know that it is your responsibility to maintain a healthy equilibrium by practicing self-care and setting healthy boundaries; it's not your sole responsibility to solve all problems or bear the emotional burdens of others. Build support networks, use stress management techniques such as mindfulness or self-reflection and seek out professional guidance if you ever feel that your empathy is becoming detrimental to your own wellbeing.

The different types of empathy

To better understand empathy, let's have a look at the three types of empathy you will encounter:

1. **Cognitive empathy** involves understanding another person's perspective on an intellectual level. For example, imagine a coworker, Alex, struggling with a heavy workload. With cognitive empathy, you can recognize and understand Alex's situation from a rational standpoint.
2. **Emotional empathy** means you can really feel what someone else is going through, not just understand it in your head. You would not only understand Alex's struggles but also experience a similar emotional response, sharing his feelings and emotional state.
3. **Compassionate empathy**, takes empathy a step further, motivating you to act and alleviate their suffering. In the case of Alex, compassionate empathy would inspire you to offer assistance, provide resources, or even lend a listening ear to help alleviate their overwhelm.

Empathy vs. Sympathy

You may be wondering at this point about the difference between sympathy and empathy, since people often use these interchangeably, not knowing exactly what each means. When you have sympathy, you will feel sorry for another's troubles or misfortunes, from a distance, and although it is often well-intended, sympathy can create distance between people, and it can lead to judgment instead of understanding. When you sympathize with someone, you may offer advice or look upon them with pity rather than truly entering their world.

When, on the other hand you have empathy, you really understand and share the other person's experiences and emotions without trying to solve or minimize them, instead, acknowledging and validating their feelings, creating a safe space where people can express themselves freely without judgment. When you show empathy, people feel heard and understood, less lonely and never judged.

What does empathy look like in the workplace?

Today's fast-paced and competitive professional environment can lead many people to believe empathy is a soft skill with no place in achieving career success. But this couldn't be further from the truth - as Tim Cook, CEO of Apple wisely put it: 'People will try convincing you not to include empathy into your career - don't succumb to this fallacy!'

Forward-thinking organizations today recognize the immense power of empathy to create positive work environments, improve collaboration, and drive employee well-being. Let's now look at empathy in the workplace using two case studies - one exemplifying empathy and one depicting the consequences of apathy.

Brandon Cook, a 21-year-old college student, faced a heart-wrenching situation when his grandmother, who was battling cancer, told him one morning that she had a craving for clam chowder from Panera Bread. Brandon was determined to fulfil her wish and he contacted the local Panera and shared his grandmother's story with the manager, Suzanne Fortier.

Despite it not being clam chowder day, Suzanne empathized with Brandon's love for his grandmother. She decided to go the extra mile, so she personally prepared the soup and surprised Brandon with a box of cookies on top, knowing that it would bring additional joy to his grandmother's day. This amazing act of kindness so touched Brandon, that he shared his experience on social media, where it quickly gained attention and support from thousands of people, proving the power of empathy in the workplace.

Apathy, on the other hand, reduces team morale, leading to decreased productivity and higher employee turnover rates. Let's look at another example and note the difference in how you feel reading this, compared to the Panera Bread situation...

A 10-year-old named Phoebe Klebahn was traveling on a United Airlines flight on her own on her way to summer camp in Chicago. She had a stopover, and being only ten years old at the time, she found herself confused about where to go. When she asked for help from United Airlines gate agents, she was met with indifference, and she was instructed to wait. Although she tried to get agents to help her, she missed her connecting flight altogether.

Phoebe's parents could not get hold of anyone to tell her what was happening, and even when they finally reached a customer service representative, that person showed no urgency and took no action. Ultimately Phoebe's parents had to insist upon speaking with a supervisor to get assistance.

What later came out was that United Airlines had a third-party agency to escort minors, like Phoebe, and although her parents paid for this service, the travel companion that was supposed to guide her never showed up. United Airlines remained unapologetic about the entire ordeal and even their response to the media outcry that followed was an emotionless response that left little comfort to anyone. I'm sure you can imagine how this plays out for any future bookings made by this family, and other families with kids.

How can you become a more empathetic leader?

We can start by acknowledging that, for most of us, empathy can be challenging because we have been trained into acting more like machines than humans!

Empathy is a powerful force that unites us through shared human experiences. Over the course of my journey spanning decades of insightful encounters, I have come to believe that no problem is too great when the right people come together.

I have found myself in meetings where progress seemed impossible; rather than giving way to frustration or despair, I have learned to remind myself, "We're missing someone essential." I have come to understand that we all yearn for that extra perspective, that spark of passion, clarity of logic, or unwavering optimism that can make all the difference in the world.

Remember, different viewpoints and the freedom to express them can break down obstacles. Humility and empathy are what let us build strength in our team. When you approach others with humility and you acknowledge your own limitations while also empathizing with their experiences and perspectives, true collaboration becomes possible.

To develop humility and empathy, we must look beyond our immediate circles to embrace diversity. While it's easy to stay close with those we already know and understand, to truly make an impactful contribution we must engage with people who think, look, or act differently from ourselves.

Empathy has an amazing power to transform situations and uplift individuals. Imagine arriving late for an appointment due to a calendar hiccup only to be met with a soothing smile and words like, 'No worries; we've all done it." At that moment, empathy creates an immediate feeling of understanding and relief for both parties involved.

Empathy and honesty

Honesty is essential in developing empathy, and it forms the basis of morality and relationship building. It requires us to acknowledge others' inherent humanity, rather than viewing them solely as objects to manipulate or avoid.

With empathy, the focus is on the other person, but honesty can serve both externally and internally, shaping our relationships and personal destinies alike. Alienation, for example, occurs when either empathy or honesty fails, and this leads to ruptured relationships and identity crises. We've already seen in the United Airlines example, how a lack of empathy disconnects us from fellow humans, undermining any chance for meaningful connections. In the same way, dishonesty with yourself compromises your own identity, you cannot know yourself if you are not honest with yourself. Similarly, when you deny someone else's experiences and humanity, you cannot see the world for what it truly is. These lies about our own and others' experiences perpetuate alienation and distance us from truth.

Let's look at another example, the company is called Exact Marketing - a fast-paced marketing agency where employees were beginning to become concerned over its financial health and rumours of potential layoffs began circulating, creating unease and anxiety among team members.

Even as their employees' anxiety rose, Exact Marketing's leadership chose not to share information, but instead maintain an appearance of stability, despite mounting suspicion. Their lack of transparency prevented open dialogue and honest communications within their teams.

As rumours swirled and employees noticed changes to project assignments and budget constraints, trust in leadership began to deteriorate. Without access to honest information, employees felt abandoned by management; thus, leading to reduced morale and productivity.

The employees couldn't understand the challenges the company was facing or understand why certain decisions had been taken and this lack of transparency created an unnecessary obstacle between leadership and employees.

Frustration mounted and employees became disengaged from their jobs, leading to a culture of suspicion and doubt that undermined collaborative efforts. Team members became more interested in protecting themselves than in teamwork or innovation. This breakdown in trust and productivity eventually led to the overall business decline.

So, once you have checked yourself for humility and honesty, (the non-negotiables), you can start implementing the following techniques to build true empathy in your workplace;

1. Display genuine concern for others and their situations: Start by recognizing each person's unique circumstances by regularly engaging in conversations with people so that you can learn about their aspirations, challenges, and personal circumstances. When you understand someone better, it becomes easier to put yourself in their shoes and feel what they are feeling.

2. Become willing to help others with personal matters: Open yourself up to not only understanding, but to the possibility of reaching out with a helping hand, to relieve their pain on a very practical level. You can start small, and always be conscious about not becoming overly involved and trying to take over the person's responsibilities. When you do this right, and you get in touch with people in this real, tangible way, you will find yourself automatically feeling more connected to them.

3: Arrange one-on-one meetings: Individual experiences are what empathy is built on, so consider setting up meetings with your team members. Select an informal location, such as a local cafe or building cafeteria to create an inviting space where the other person feels safe enough to discuss their emotions freely. This is especially important when you are meeting with someone where there is an unequal relationship of power, like an employee / employer relationship. One-on-one meetings like this can help you gain valuable insights into the wellbeing and concerns of that person.

4: Monitor work burnout: To be an empathetic leader, you must become attentive to any signs of work burnout among your team members. What does this mean, practically? To monitor burnout, look for signs of stress, like exhaustion or disengagement in behaviour. When you have your finger on the pulse of possible burnout, you will be able to intervene and give any necessary support, promoting work-life balance or even redistribute tasks among teammates to reduce the risks or prevent burnout entirely in all your team members.

5. Use employee analytics: Today, more than ever, you can use the power of data to gain insights into your team's well-being. For example, you can send happiness and engagement surveys (check out https://thehappinessindex.com/) for real-time feedback from employees. With this data, you can assess overall team mood, identify areas of concern, and focus your leadership efforts more effectively. By guaranteeing anonymous feedback, this data can help encourage more open communication.

Quick tips to a more empathetic you…

Reflect: Take time to assess how empathetic you are. Think about whether you understand and relate to other's emotions and experiences effectively and remember that self-reflection is an essential step in developing empathy.

Prioritize people: Express genuine interest in people's needs, hopes, and aspirations while offering support when someone shares personal challenges or tragedies.

Practice perspective-taking: Put yourself in another person's shoes and try to listen not only to what they have said but also take note of their tone of voice and body language, try to understand, and express their feelings and emotions using your own language.

Engage in meaningful conversations: Go beyond digital communication and make time for face-to-face talks, rather than only relying on instant messages or email.

Explore new experiences: Open yourself up to new experiences by participating in activities that broaden your understanding of other people's perspectives.

Take feedback seriously: Actively seek feedback on your empathy levels from others on a regular basis, specifically finding out where you can improve.

Daily empathy practices: Make empathy part of your daily practice, taking small steps to demonstrate it with colleagues, friends, and family members. Actively listen, validate emotions when appropriate, and offer support (not solutions), wherever possible.

Emotional Intelligence

Of course, empathy is only the starting step, the foundation if you will – and the immediate skill you can begin to build on is emotional intelligence or "EQ". Emotional intelligence accounts for nearly 90% of what sets high performers apart from peers with similar technical skills and knowledge.

What is emotional intelligence, and why does it matter?

The term emotional intelligence or EQ was first coined by John Mayer and Peter Salovey in 1990, and it is defined as the ability to understand and manage your own emotions, as well as recognize and influence the emotions of those around you.

Emotional intelligence is typically broken down into four core competencies, these are:

Self-awareness, as already touched upon, refers to your ability to understand your strengths and weaknesses and recognize your emotions and their effect on you and your team's performance.

While 95% of people think they're self-aware, only 10 to 15 percent actually are. This is a great opportunity because you can potentially double your team's performance, reducing stress and increasing motivation by helping them increase their self-awareness. To do this, you must first make sure *you* are self-aware.

Self-management, is about managing your emotions, especially in stressful situations. It is also about being able to stay positive despite setbacks and remain calm under pressure.

When you are in tune with your emotions, you can start responding instead of merely reacting. The way to do this is to pause, breathe, collect yourself, and do whatever it takes to manage your emotions before you respond, more about this later, when we look at mindfulness as a way to cultivate emotional intelligence.

Social awareness, is about knowing how to read a room and recognizing other people's emotions and dynamics, as well as understanding other people's feelings and perspectives.

Relationship management, refers to your ability to influence, coach, and mentor others, as well as resolve conflict effectively. Every unaddressed conflict drains a business's resources and morale; it is estimated that every such issue can waste about eight hours of company time in gossip and other unproductive activities.

72% percent of employees ranked "respectful treatment of all employees at all levels" as the top factor in job satisfaction in a recent Society for Human Resource Management survey. For this very reason, IQ and technical skills are now seen as merely the entry-level requirements for executive positions; they are no longer sufficient for success. In fact, 71% of employers surveyed by CareerBuilder said they value EQ over IQ.

Emotional intelligence and leadership

When I started doing research on emotional intelligence, I was surprised to find out that only about 36 percent of people can accurately identify their emotions as they happen. The trouble is that, since leaders set the tone of their organization, when they lack emotional intelligence, it siphons through to the rest of the organization, causing lower employee engagement and higher turnover rates, typically due to toxic interactions between people.

If you find that you frequently have challenging interactions with others, you find people difficult, and you don't really understand that others are part of the equation, it may be time to take a closer look at your emotional intelligence, because these may be signs that you need some work in this area.

What does emotional intelligence at the workplace look like?

To better understand emotional intelligence, and how it can impact teams, let's use an example, based on a hypothetical scenario where a leader with high emotional intelligence is brought in, and the effect that can have on turning around the business.

To recap, Exact Marketing's team had become disengaged over time due to a lack of honesty and transparency and years of being treated like mere cogs in an assembly line, without consideration given for emotions or well-being. In this business, a culture of disengagement had developed, leaving team members feeling undervalued and distant from each other.

Now let's imagine a new CEO taking over the reins, we will call him George, an emotionally mature servant leader with an excellent track record, who is brought in by investors to turn things around. Let's imagine his journey and explore how one strong leader can turn things around:

As soon as George walks into the office on his first day, he immediately senses the team's distrust; however, he is not at all thrown by this as he expected it. With what the team had just been through, it is only natural that it will take some time to rebuild trust and build a collaborative and inclusive work environment.

George convenes an office meeting, gathering all his new team members around a large conference table. He can feel their past experiences weighing down on them, a palpable tension that needs to be addressed directly. With a deep breath in, he begins setting the agenda.

"Thank you all for coming today," he states with genuine warmth and sincerity. "I want you all to know that I am fully dedicated to creating an exceptional workplace - one in which empathy, honesty, collaboration, and growth form the basis of everything we do."

The team exchange glances, curious yet cautious. George continues to speak about his professional journey, lessons learned, and values that guide his leadership style. He speaks openly and transparently, being vulnerable in front of his new team.

As the meeting continues, George uses active listening - a skill he has perfected over time - to ensure every team member can express their thoughts and concerns without fear of being judged. Each heartfelt story and candid revelation create a safe space for open dialogue that transforms into productive discussions.

George is quick to show his empathy as he acknowledges the impact of previous leadership's influence on the morale and well-being among team members. *"I understand your frustrations and the need for change,"* he tells them, his eyes meeting theirs with understanding. *"We are all human with emotions and aspirations - it's time we built an environment which recognizes this."*

Transparency and honesty have long been George's guiding life principles. He addresses any team concerns head-on while addressing the issues of financial stability in the company. He makes it clear that he will never avoid tough conversations or withhold information that may affect the work and the lives of the people in the room.

George strongly believes that collaborative problem-solving is the foundation of effective leadership, he engages his team members asking for their inputs on communication strategies, work-life balance initiatives, and ways to create an inclusive and supportive workplace culture. Together with his team, they collaborate on co-creating a roadmap for change.

He doesn't stop there, though - his open-door policy becomes more than just an empty phrase, he proves over time that he is available to his team members, and he makes time for important conversations, one-on-one.

Over time, George's leadership, emotional intelligence, and empathy help the once apathetic team to change, slowly but steadily rebuilding trust until finally they no longer see themselves as mere employees but as unique individuals with unique talents and aspirations working toward one common goal.

Increasing your EQ

The rewards of high emotional intelligence are plentiful, not only for your professional life but also for your relationships and mental, emotional, and even physical health. But how do you become more emotionally intelligent? or is it something you are born with?

The good news is that you can develop emotional intelligence. As with matters of the heart, it is not a black-and-white process, and you may have to employ several techniques and practices to grow your emotional intelligence over time. The first step in this journey is to identify and master your "triggers" and "signs."

"Triggers" are the people, scenarios, and topics that can set your emotions off: Your manager publicly criticizes your presentation, you get another round of unrealistic deadlines for multiple projects, or you realize that your hard work on a challenging project went unnoticed and unacknowledged by your superiors.

"Signs," on the other hand, are the physical manifestations of negative emotions you feel. After your manager publicly criticizes your presentation, you feel defensive, hurt, and frustrated. You may flush red in the face, feel sweat on your palms, bite your lip to stop it quivering or simply feel an urge to scream, run or hide.

Once you have become aware of your triggers and signs, the next step is to learn to manage them. This can be easier said than done because, as the science of attachment indicates, your current emotional experience is likely a reflection of your early life experience, meaning that your ability to manage big feelings like anger, sadness, fear, and joy often depends on the quality and consistency of your early life emotional experiences. If, for example, your primary caretaker as a child understood and valued your emotions, it's likely your emotions have become valuable assets in adult life. But, if your emotional experiences as a young child were confusing, threatening, or painful, you've probably tried to distance yourself from your emotions.

That being said, building a moment-to-moment connection with your changing emotional experience is the key to understanding how emotion influences your thoughts and actions, and it is entirely possible, even if you grew up with emotional neglect.

You need to become friends with your emotions, facing each of your experiences and calmly acknowledging the changes in your emotional state from moment to moment. How do you do this? Start by taking note of the physical sensations you feel in places like your stomach, throat, or chest, this will help you identify and manage your emotions. For example, a burning sensation on your abdomen usually indicates fear, while a clenching feeling in your heart area can indicate sadness.

When you don't yet know your emotions, you will just feel 'bad' or 'good,' and as you become more familiar with your state, and you learn to differentiate between the different sensations in your body and mind, you will begin to distinguish individual feelings and emotions, such as anger, sadness, fear, and joy, from each other. Once you can do this, you can begin to manage these emotions, and you can see how they affect your decision-making, which will, in turn, help you make better quality decisions, as you are no longer blindly led by your feelings.

But how do you actually connect with emotions?
Mindfulness is the answer to this. Mindfulness is the practice of purposely focusing your attention on the present moment without judgment; to some people, this is known as meditating. Meditating helps shift you from being caught up in random thoughts toward a real-time appreciation of the moment. It calms and focuses you, making you more self-aware in the process.

Quick tips for growing your emotional intelligence

Apart from practicing mindfulness and managing your triggers and signs, there are some additional and practical ways to help you display emotional intelligence in your day-to-day environment:

- Keep a productive and positive tone when you address people.
- Focus on positive body language. (Smile, don't fidget, stand, or sit up straight, avoid crossing your arms or legs etc.)

- Step back and assess issues objectively, take a breather when you feel yourself losing control of your emotions.
- Use open-ended probes like, *"Tell me more about that"* or *"Help me understand"* to ensure that you understand the other person's point of view.
- Actively manage your stress levels. (Practise deep breathing techniques, get daily exercise or at least fresh air, eat a healthy diet etc.)
- Stay emotionally present. (Limit distractions, stay in the now.)
- Take time to consider the other person's motivations.
- Assume positive intent in others, in other words, expect the best from them.
- Use humour and play to relieve tension; these are natural antidotes to stress.
- Encourage laughter; it brings your nervous system into balance, reducing stress, calming you down, sharpening your mind, and making you more empathetic.
- Learn to see conflict as an opportunity to grow closer to others. Resolving conflict in healthy, constructive ways can strengthen trust between people, and when conflict isn't perceived as threatening or punishing, it promotes freedom, creativity, and safety in relationships.

As we close this discussion on the emotional skills you need, we turn our attention to leading effectively because, to be a leader, you need to actually lead.

So, let's get started on becoming a strategic leader, one who knows what their vision is and can communicate it to others...

Chapter 7 - Think Like a Leader

"The power of thought, —the magic of the mind!"

- Lord Byron,
The Corsair,
Canto I, Stanza 8

In this chapter, we will look at **strategy** and **vision**, the next tools in our arsenal against IS, and some of the most important elements of a successful life, career, and business.

What is Strategy?

Imagine yourself as the captain of a ship, using strategic thinking as your compass to plot a course through uncharted waters. Strategic thinking helps uncover hidden treasures and steer the vessel towards success, not simply making plans but instead unlocking unique opportunities that can bring immense value to your organization. Consider this: on board are crew members from various walks of life, each having different experiences and perspectives that hold key insights which could revolutionize your voyage.

The word "strategy" has its roots in ancient Greek. It derives from the Greek word "strategia," which is a combination of "stratos" meaning "army" or "military" and "agein" meaning "to lead" or "to guide." A person with strategic thinking can think systematically, considering all the factors and calculating probabilities.

Strategic thinking is not exclusive to a select few in high positions; anyone, from the newest recruit to an experienced deckhand, can incorporate strategic thinking into their thought processes. Anyone could be sitting on crucial information, game-changing ideas, or simple inquiries that unlock unexpected solutions and pave the way to long-term success.

Remember the conversations about empathy, emotional intelligence, and diversity? These factors form the backbone of strategic thinking. The more viewpoints and perspectives you bring on board, the greater will be your creative output and energy. Imagine harnessing all that collective brainpower that a diverse crew brings.

As we move forward, let's distinguish strategic planning from strategic thinking. Planning is like plotting your course on a map based on information available at one moment in time - leaders gather data and decide the course for the organization. However, strategic thinking involves constantly scanning the horizon in search of new ways to contribute and propel its success, creating an environment in which every crew member feels empowered to think strategically while producing ideas and innovations that keep you all sailing smoothly.

Strategic thinking cannot be overemphasized: without it, your crew could drift aimlessly and disengage from one another in an uncertain world. But when strategic thinking thrives, amazing things can happen.

To demonstrate the real-life value of strategic thinking done well, I have summarised three case studies from big businesses that got it right.

Amazon's Innovation in Online Shopping:

Amazon was challenged with changing the online shopping experience beyond offering competitive prices. Their solution involved revamping shopping procedures with concepts like Sunday delivery and drone drop-offs that enhanced convenience and speed when purchasing items online. They gained an edge by investing in innovative customer experiences such as Amazon Prime subscriptions that eliminated shipping costs - establishing themselves as an e-commerce leader and giving themselves an advantage in competitive situations.

Use of Celebrity Endorsements by Nike

Nike's success through strategic brand positioning, innovative design, and social media marketing efforts demonstrates strategic thinking on a number of levels already, but their use of celebrity endorsements stands out for me as one of their most successful ideas.

Over the years, Nike has partnered with prominent athletes and celebrities to endorse its products. This not only enhances the brand's credibility but also connects it with consumers who admire and aspire to be like these figures.

Quality Management at Apple Inc.

Apple recognized that product quality and customer satisfaction were primary differentiators in their market space; both were a challenge in their organization. So, Apple prioritized quality management above everything else by investing in reliable products with extensive warranties and support resources. Their strategic focus on quality and customer support generated extreme customer loyalty among those willing to pay more for such features.

How can you become a strategic thinker?

Once you understand the true value of strategic thinking, you may ask yourself how you can become better at strategic thinking yourself. The answer lies in you, or to be more specific, in your perspective. You must understand your perspective first and have a good view of your personal story and experiences.

The challenge is that most of us do not know ourselves well enough to be able to put into words what this perspective is, so below, I have laid out a 5-point plan to help you identify and articulate your personal perspective. I suggest taking out your notebook and spending some time thinking about each point. This exercise will not only help you start strategic thinking on your current core challenge (more about that later), but it will serve you in strategic thinking for the rest of your career and life.

1. **List Influential Factors:** Start by compiling a list of influential factors. These could be books, courses, speeches, or movies, that had a lasting effect on you. Current "You-Tubers", podcasters and authors who shape your thinking and provide valuable guidance and perspective.

2. **Consider Your Experiences:** Take time to pause and reflect upon the experiences that have shaped your understanding of who you are, where you came from, and your aspirations for the future. Your individual journey adds depth and richness to your perspective. Try taking it a decade at a time, from birth, listing both positive and negative experiences for each decade.

3. **Explore Near-Death Experiences or Traumatic Events:** Challenges or obstacles can provide profound lessons; Christopher Columbus survived both pirate attacks and

shipwrecks to gain valuable insights into exploration. Reflecting upon your own near-death experiences or traumatic events may give you a unique lens through which to view life.

4. **Consider how others see you:** Think carefully about how you want others to perceive you - this is your personal brand; imagine the reputation you would like others to associate with you. When you leave a room, what words would you want people to use when talking about you?

5. **Assess Moral Righteousness:** Take time to reflect upon your moral values and principles, for these are the basis of your decisions and actions. Aligning your strategy with these deeply held beliefs allows you to navigate life with integrity.

The next step is to recognise the value of the perspective you have just uncovered. Your unique experiences and insights have shaped the lens through which you see the world, and you can now begin to use that perspective to your advantage; it can become a strategic asset. Let's look at how you can do that.

Imagine living in a world where everyone shares the exact same perception of reality, accepting its status quo without question. Now imagine you have the gift of "contrarian thought" (opposing viewpoints or "thinking-outside-the-box"). By challenging conventional wisdom and taking an alternative stance, you have an incredible power to identify opportunities and creative solutions that others miss. Say you are participating in a team brainstorming session where everyone seems to be heading in one direction; by taking an independent perspective, you could uncover unexpected solutions and breakthroughs that others might overlook. Your contrarian perspective allows you to question assumptions, propose alternate strategies, and lead your team toward innovative ideas.

Contrary to popular opinion, Steve Jobs of Apple challenged the prevailing notion that larger was better in technology by creating the smartphone revolution. By unveiling their groundbreaking device - iPhone with its touchscreen interface and app ecosystem - Jobs forever altered how we communicate and access information.

If you are like me, you might question yourself when you have an idea that others are not mentioning; you might assume that it is not a valid idea because if it were, someone else would have mentioned it. When this happens, try to remember the lessons about perspective, it is entirely possible that no one else is thinking of your idea simply because no one else has your exact perspective, so don't lose the power of your unique perspective by failing to share it. Instead, embrace its potential and use your voice to disrupt the mundane.

The power of courage: As you begin the journey of strategic thinking, courage becomes your constant companion. Successful strategists have the audacity to take calculated risks, make bold decisions and challenge the status quo, but doing so means venturing beyond your comfort zone into uncharted territories. When you are faced with uncertainty, your courage will help push you toward change, seizing opportunities, or adopting unconventional strategies - remember it takes strength to stand apart especially when others may doubt or resist your vision.

Take, for example, Rosa Parks, who inspired the Montgomery Bus Boycott during the civil rights movement by refusing to give up her seat on a segregated bus and challenging the discriminatory norms of her time. Her strategic act (whether intentional or unintentional) triggered a widespread change that ultimately transformed how we fight for equality today

161

Coherence is key: Your perspective must be organized into logical, coherent, and aligned thoughts, ideas, and actions. Doing this allows you to ensure your strategies have strong justification behind them, enabling you to clearly see the bigger picture at all times.

Look at Elon Musk, the visionary entrepreneur behind Tesla and SpaceX. His holistic perspective on sustainable energy and space exploration drives his strategic decisions; electric vehicle production and renewable energy initiatives align perfectly with his goal of creating a cleaner future through renewables, regardless of the challenges thrown his way.

Common sense will prevail: Your common-sense perspective will provide clarity in an otherwise confusing world, making decisions with practical reasoning and sound judgment, relying on intuition as much as possible, supported with the necessary experience and knowledge.

Warren Buffett, for example, is one of the most successful investors alive today. He is known for his grounded approach to investing. Instead of getting distracted by media hype or general sentiment about an assets' worth, Buffett prefers analysing fundamental value, competitive edge, and potential growth of companies he invests in - this straightforward approach has guided his wise investment decisions such as Coca-Cola and See's Candies investments that have yielded stunning returns over time. Buffett reminds us all that sometimes simple solutions can be the most effective.

Perspective and the Core Challenge - tying it together

Within every person and every organization lies a core challenge. That pivotal obstacle that, once it is overcome, holds the key to future success. The essence of a successful strategy lies in understanding and addressing this core challenge. This sounds simple, right? Identify the core challenge and strategize around it. Why then are we not better at doing this all the time? The challenge is that we often find ourselves fighting fires and addressing urgent matters, and we get so caught up that we don't get to the important work, the work of pinpointing our core challenges, so that we can strategize for them.

To be successful in strategic thinking, you need to break free from this cycle of firefighting, and in this section, we will explore the power of identifying and embracing your core challenge.

Defining the Core Challenge: Let's say you are a talented professional who aspires to advance your career. Your core challenge may be the lack of effective networking skills and a limited professional network. However, you may be so focused on improving your technical expertise or day-to-day job performance that you overlook this core challenge.
If you take the time to identify your core challenge, you might refocus some of your energy toward building valuable connections and expanding your influence. This strategic shift will make all the difference in your career and life trajectory.

The truth is that many of us shy away from truly understanding our core challenge. We tend to avoid unpleasant truths and brush aside problems that demand action. By neglecting to define the core challenge, we remain trapped in a cycle of reactive problem-solving, never reaching the strategic breakthrough we desire. Only by recognizing and addressing this core challenge question head-on can we take the first steps towards developing strategies to solve it and reach our full potential.

You may, from time to time, find yourself stuck in a chicken-and-egg situation where addressing either your ctrategic perspective or core challenge first is confusing; where do you start, and which do you take care of first? To get out of this rut of confusion, I suggest taking an integrated approach that allows you to look at both questions simultaneously.

Imagine, for example, you are an aspiring entrepreneur wanting to launch an innovative product; your strategy reveals a keen focus on sustainability and commitment to environmentally friendly solutions. At the same time, you recognize your core challenge: the lack of financial resources necessary for realizing your idea.

Now, if you take the time to put the two threads together, it becomes clear that your strategy must prioritize developing innovative funding models, engaging with impact investors, and emphasizing sustainability as a unique selling point. By adopting such an integrated approach, both perspectives can inform each other, resulting in an approach tailored to fit your values and goals.

I invite you to take some time and consider your strategic perspective and challenges in depth. What obstacles stand between you and achieving your desired success? How have unique insights or experiences shaped your perspective? Take time for self-exploration; that may just be what unlocks strategic brilliance.

In my own journey I have found my own "Law of 5" for successful strategic brilliance;

1. **Step out of your comfort zone:** Explore industries or cultures different from yours to observe problem-solving approaches.
2. **Engage with different people:** Seek informal conversations with individuals knowledgeable about your situation or issue.

3. **Challenge assumptions:** Identify and question assumptions related to causes, options, and the environment to increase the chances of success.
4. **Connect with the past:** Draw parallels from similar situations that occurred in the past to gain insights.
5. **Expect the unexpected:** Imagine future scenarios where your plan fails, identify potential risks, and devise strategies to mitigate them.

Strategic thinking has the potential to transform your approach to problem-solving and decision-making. If you are willing to step out of your comfort zone and embrace the techniques in this section, you will develop the strategic mindset that you need to help you tackle the challenges on your path with confidence and absolute clarity.

Talking of clarity, strategic thinking requires you to have a clear vision of what you want to achieve, either with your team, the project you are leading or managing, or the goal of your organization. So, let's look at the concept of vision next.

Vision

To get back the example of the ship, we have discussed the idea that strategy decides HOW to get the ship across the waters, the next big question is - WHERE is the ship headed. It is one of the primary tasks of a leader to become crystal clear on the destination, the Vision - because once you can align teams around a shared vision - sailing becomes much, much smoother

What is Vision?

A leader's vision inspires and unifies, creating a shared dream and a path that employees willingly embrace and follow. Vision, simply put, is the ultimate destination that a leader strives to reach, channelling their energy and resources towards its realization. It is defined as "**a clearly articulated view of the future**".

Behind every thriving organization, there is a concise and widely understood vision that directs the actions and behaviour of every person in the organization. A leader's vision guides the organization's strategy by aligning all areas towards a common goal, reducing ambiguity, and providing focus, particularly in turbulent or rapidly changing times.

Leadership vision extends beyond merely written mission and vision statements. It is reflected in the actions, beliefs, and values its leaders demonstrate.

Why is vision important?

A clear and well-communicated vision is essential for a leader to gain support, build trust, and for followers to gain understanding. It is an internal driving force that compels leaders to act, providing them with a purpose and direction. Even when facing challenges and obstacles, a steadfast vision empowers leaders to progress.

The importance of having a shared vision cannot be overstated.
According to John Kotter, the vision of an organization serves three main purposes:

- It clarifies the general direction of change, which makes life easier later while change is happening.
- It motivates individuals to take action in the right direction, even if there's internal conflict or discomfort.
- It coordinates the actions of everyone involved, which makes the entire operation more efficient and cost-effective.

One of the most powerful aspects of a clear vision is that it can create a sense of ownership among employees. The pronoun "our" replaces "company," instilling a greater level of engagement, motivation, and personal investment in the work. Employees find greater meaning and purpose in their roles by working towards a shared vision. This becomes a magnet for top talent seeking to be part of something larger than themselves.

What happens when vision fails?

"If there is no vision, people cannot survive." This holds in both business and life. Leaders without a clear vision operate in a stagnant and repetitive way. Without a core purpose, values, and vision, the company, as promising as it may be, is headed toward dead end after dead end. It's just not going to work.

Case study: Leadership Vision Failure at Yahoo: The Marissa Mayer era

This case study explores the leadership challenges that Marissa Mayer faced during her tenure as CEO of Yahoo. Despite her initial promise, her inability to deliver a compelling vision for the company's revival resulted in missed opportunities and a failure to regain market dominance.

Background:
In March 2013, concerns were raised about Marissa Mayer's suitability for the CEO role at Yahoo due to her lack of leadership experience. It was evident from the outset that she faced a formidable task in reviving a company struggling to adapt to a rapidly changing industry landscape. However, the Yahoo board failed to recognize these leadership deficiencies and overlooked the potential consequences of their decision.

Mayer inherited a company burdened by an outdated business model and a tarnished brand reputation. A clear and inspiring vision was critical to rally the organization. However, Mayer's decision-making record was plagued by questionable choices, hindering Yahoo's progress at every turn. Her leadership style emphasized personal interests over the team's well-being and failed to inspire trust and confidence.

Impact on Organizational Culture:
Under Mayer's leadership, Yahoo's corporate culture deteriorated significantly. The toxic environment bred mistrust, stifled innovation, and hindered collaboration among employees. Mayer's lack of understanding and neglect of the delicate interdependencies within the company's culture resulted in a missed opportunity to leverage culture as a performance accelerator.

Lessons Learned:
The importance of selecting a leader with the appropriate skills and experience for the role is apparent. Mayer's lack of leadership capabilities hindered Yahoo's ability to thrive in a highly competitive industry.

Building trust across all levels of the organization is crucial for success. Mayer's failure to establish trust and engage with the workforce hampered employee motivation and productivity.

Understanding and nurturing organizational culture is vital. Mayer's inability to comprehend the underlying mechanisms of Yahoo's culture prevented her from effecting meaningful change and inhibiting the toxic environment that had developed.

Placing team interests above personal ambitions is a hallmark of effective leadership. Mayer's self-focused approach alienated employees and hindered their contributions to the company's success.

This case study is a cautionary tale for organizations regarding the consequences of a leader's failure to deliver a compelling vision. Mayer's shortcomings, coupled with the oversight of the Yahoo board, resulted in missed opportunities for revival.

In the following sections, we will explore practical strategies and exercises to help you cultivate and nurture your own leadership vision.

What does a clear vision look like?

Since the concept of a vision is somewhat abstract by nature, there is no exact recipe for creating a winning vision, and as companies innovate, and come up with ideas and methods that have never been seen before, the concept of what a vision can be is ever-changing. That being said, there are some guidelines you can use to make sure your vision is well crafted and likely to be well understood and received. Here are some key qualities of a well-crafted vision:

- It is grounded in logic and reason.
- It is reasonable and realistically attainable.
- It is innovative.
- It is credible.
- It is clearly articulated and easily understood by everyone.
- It is motivating and stimulating.
- It is challenging.
- It reflects the beliefs, values, and culture of the organization.
- It is concrete, tangible, and leaves no room for ambiguity.

As you consider the vision for your life or your business, keep this list at hand and check yourself that you are ticking off all these points. As you become more and more experienced in crafting a vision, it will become more natural, but for the first few attempts you may need to make edits and go back to the drawing board several times. It is also a good idea to get a trusted mentor or friend to help you evaluate your vision against these points, to ensure you are objective when creating your vision.

How to develop a vision

Simon Sinek's Golden Circle provides an easy, three-step formula any company can use to ignite action by starting with "Why." Based on the golden ratio and the human brain's natural functions, this strategy uses purpose to instigate action from their audience and meet basic human needs. Consisting of three concentric circles - Why, How, and What - the innermost circle represents the purpose or belief driving leadership or organizations and provides a sense of belonging and 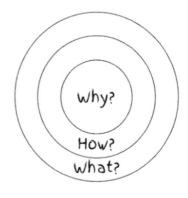 fulfilment; the middle circle shows the unique approach or value proposition provided; the outermost circle details products or services offered.

Let's look at the three circles individually.

Find your "Why"

To lead with purpose and motivate others, it is vital that you recognize the "Why" behind your organization. Your "Why" represents your reason for existing, and the source of all your actions.

Belonging is a basic human need, and when people feel connected to a cause or organization, they feel a sense of safety. People actively seek communities to devote themselves to and make an impactful contribution - sometimes people even go so far as getting tattooed with a logo to symbolize an identity greater than themselves!

How to get to "Why"

To get to your "Why" may be quite a journey, take the time to uncover your own thoughts, beliefs, and ambitions. You can use the tools that I mentioned earlier in the book to get to know yourself better and once you understand your motives, you can answer that crucial question: "Why am I doing this?".

Here are some questions and contemplations you can use to help you get to your reason for leading your team:

What is your collective cause or belief, and why is it relevant to the business?
Think about what motivates the organization as a whole; its overarching purpose should reflect the changes you want to see in society as well as your values.

Are you seeking a brighter vision of tomorrow?
Imagine the ideal future you want your work to create and identify how your organization will contribute towards this positive transformation. Identify specific actions which align with this vision and bring it closer to reality.

How can your business's purpose help your customers achieve their own purpose?
Consider how the mission and objectives of your organization align with those of its target audience, specifically customers in its target demographic. How does your "Why" intertwine with their needs, desires, or goals?

Who do your clients belong to?
Learn to understand what group or community your clients seek to join and how your organization can provide this experience for them. By aligning your values and aspirations

with those of your customers, you create a tribe of like-minded individuals who resonate with your "Why".

How do you make it happen?

Once you've determined your "Why", the next step should be identifying the "How": how will your organization fulfil its mission and meet its purpose?

Simon Sinek defines "How" as your organization's differentiating value proposition, proprietary process, or unique selling proposition. This aspect embodies everything that makes your organization distinct in the eyes of customers and stakeholders. While your "Why" represents its overarching purpose or belief; "How" addresses practical steps taken to bring this belief to life.

To discover your business's "How", keep these factors in mind:

What does your company do to set itself apart?
Consider all the aspects that set your organization apart from competitors in its industry. What unique features, qualities, or offerings make your organization shine above its peers? Identify areas where your organization excels and utilize those resources as competitive advantages.
Take some time to reflect upon the unique value and significance of your organization. What distinguishes it from others in its industry? Do its products, services, or initiatives make a meaningful difference in people's lives - customers, stakeholders, or the larger community?

Which exciting developments motivate employees and customers?
Take time to identify which innovations, breakthroughs, or developments spark enthusiasm among both your staff and customers alike. Examining what exciting technologies or developments drive your industry forward can spark energy

and motivation within your team while drawing in like-minded individuals who appreciate its progressive nature.

Where does your organization create value?

Determine which areas or aspects of your organization provide the greatest benefit to customers, stakeholders, or the community. This may be achieved through exceptional quality products or services, unparalleled support, unique expertise, or even a transformative experience. Understand which ways your influence positively affects others' lives and then work on strengthening these aspects further.

What could impact decision-making?

Consider all the elements that play into customers' and stakeholders' decision-making. What are their needs, pain points, desires, or wants that need to be addressed by your organization in an engaging manner? By understanding and aligning with their decision-making criteria, you can craft an approach that resonates with them and grabs their attention.

Contemplate these considerations and uncover your organization's individual "How". Create strategies that draw upon its strengths to outwit competitors and remember that your "How" should always align with and support your "Why" so that every action and decision you take is purposeful.

Implement your "How" into every aspect of your organization - from product development to customer service and marketing. Be clear and consistent in communicating the distinct advantages and benefits that your organization offers its customers or stakeholders, creating a compelling narrative that resonates with them. You will strengthen loyalty to your brand.

What exactly is it that you do?

At the core of every organization's journey lies its "What", which refers to tangible and visible components of its business. Most businesses understand their "What" well enough that it often serves as their guidepost when operating from the outside in. It includes products, services, actions, and responsibilities that define daily operations, driving rational decision-making processes, while your "Why" and "How" address heartfelt emotion.

Consider these key elements when creating the "What" for your organization:

What products or services do you sell?
Clearly define the products or services your organization provides, outlining tangible offerings that customers can expect from you and outline any core features, benefits, and unique selling points which set them apart in the marketplace.

What steps is the company taking to turn its "Why" into reality?
Explore what actions and initiatives your organization takes. to bring its "Why" into existence. How do you accomplish your mission and put into practice your beliefs in real-world scenarios? Identify strategic decisions, processes, and activities that drive its goals forward while contributing meaningfully towards creating a brighter future.

Recognize that individuals in your organization play vital roles in fulfilling its purpose. Determine what roles employees take on to contribute to the collective mission - from leaders to frontline workers; everyone has their part to play. Clarify how each role connects to "Why", "How", and "What" to emphasize each employee's contributions toward reaching a shared vision.

By clearly outlining your organization's "What," you will establish a solid base that supports and reinforces its "Why" and "How". Be sure that this aligns with your core beliefs and values. Communicate this "What" consistently, both internally and externally, to create a shared understanding and gain trust among stakeholders.

Completing the Golden Circle

Implementing the golden circle, the coming together of your Why, How, and What, can have a dramatic effect on the communication of your brand within any organization. Apple is a prime example of leading with "Why", inspiring their audiences through purpose-driven messaging. Under Steve Jobs' direction, Apple used this method to craft a brand that resonated deeply with its target market.

Most businesses tend to emphasize their "What" and "How" instead of their "Why". Apple broke away from this when it ran its 1997 "Think Different" ad featuring its late iconic leader, Steve Jobs. The campaign stood out due to its focus on "Why" rather than its products or calls to action - standing as an inspirational tribute for those who dared to think differently.

Instead of communicating its mission of "We make great computers that are beautifully designed, simple to use, and user-friendly - would anyone like one?", Apple went further. They conveyed their core belief of challenging the status quo and thinking differently with products designed specifically to support that mission - creating a sense of belonging among customers who share those ideals and encouraging customers who support nonconformist ideals to buy their products.

A textbook example: Airbnb

Airbnb gave us an impressive example of a company that effectively leads with its "Why", emphasizing customers' primal need for belonging. Instead of simply renting houses, their core message focuses on home and belonging. According to co-founder Brian Chesky, while houses may serve a practical function, home is where one truly belongs - this understanding sets them apart and guides their brand.

Airbnb consistently communicates its message of belonging across its brand touchpoints. Their mission statement encapsulates it: creating a world where people can feel at home no matter where they reside versus just traveling to it. By emphasizing its centrality to life, Airbnb differentiates itself from other rental platforms by emphasizing its purpose rather than explicitly outlining its "What".

Airbnb's dedication to its "Why" can be seen through initiatives like OpenHomes. Since 2012, they have worked with over 50,000 refugees and individuals in need by providing free accommodation through this initiative - showing their mission extends far beyond renting homes!

Follow Airbnb's example and use your "Why" to create an engaging brand for your audience. Focusing on the core purpose, and understanding its broader impact will differentiate your business and create deeper customer connections.

Communicating your Vision

Once carefully articulated, your vision should now be clearly communicated to attract an audience who is not only familiar with your vision but willing to support it too.

Opening this dialogue and then listening to the reactions permits you to gauge if others share similar concerns, perhaps ones that you had experienced when crafting it, whether it is easy to understand, and it provides invaluable feedback that you can use to strengthen your vision.

You should also include your why in your communications. One way to do this is to add "because" before each statement.

For example, when stating, "We need to improve our process because ___," you directly address the motivation and justification for taking an action you propose. By clearly communicating why they need to improve, others can gain greater insight into your request.

Answering "why" questions with empathy and sensitivity adds an effective, persuasive edge to your communication. By offering clear rationales and addressing potential concerns, you will forge deeper relationships and engagement between customers and employees alike.

Once your vision and goals have been clearly articulated, you should create an action plan and operational strategies to fulfil them. Your vision and goals must align with structures, cultures, and operations. I suggest breaking annual goals down into 90-day objectives as this helps maintain momentum as you work toward new ones every three months, or better still take a look at the "12 Week Year" by Brian P Moran, a concept I switched to some time ago and have never looked back.

Once your thoughts are aligned, your vision has been shared and people are motivated by it, you can now use it as a force for action. In the next chapter, we'll unpack this crucial step in detail.

Chapter 8 - Act Like a Leader

---

*"I have always thought the actions of men
the best interpreters of their thoughts."*

- John Locke,
An Essay Concerning Human Understanding,
Book 1, Chapter 3, Section 3

Goal setting

In the words of John F. Kennedy, "Effort and courage are not enough without purpose and direction."

By my early thirties, I was typically doing 10–12-hour workdays in corporate, and whilst I enjoyed my work and found it at least somewhat meaningful, I found myself thinking that I was not made to do that forever. I knew I needed to do something to get out of the corporate rat race; working for a salary until retirement was not what I wanted to do with my life. It was not my purpose.

I had heard many stories of great entrepreneurs who started their businesses under the same circumstances. They were working full-time jobs and came up with great ideas that fulfilled a need in the market. Their ventures went from strength to strength, and over time, they grew. They could eventually leave their office job, become involved in their side venture full-time, and grow their business into a thriving enterprise. Soon enough, they would start employing people, making healthy profits, and ultimately have control over their own time and, importantly, take the profits for themselves instead of making an employer rich.

This became my dream. I spent hours and hours looking for the right opportunity, testing ideas in my mind, running SWOT analyses in my free time, and dreaming of financial freedom, but never taking steps to get there, that's because what I should have been doing was turning my dreams into actual goals. Manageable, realistic goals.

Goal setting keeps you focused on what really matters. It allows you to establish a larger picture or vision that you strive for, acting as a guideline when prioritizing tasks and keeping order in your world. Setting SMART goals will help you set clear targets for where your efforts and that of your team should go. It will help you avoid acting irrationally in the face of trouble and worrying over minor problems as you come to understand that these little problems won't significantly impact your long-term goals.
Setting goals also allows you to prioritize your health and personal well-being because when you have a clear view of your long-term goals, you can acknowledge the worth of your wellness in the grand scheme of things.

Goal setting gives leaders constant motivation. A sense of purpose to keep your commitment and drive strong for months and years to come. As a leader, you need this because, unlike employees, you may not receive much external motivation. Setting ambitious, compelling, and seemingly impossible (yet realistic) goals will help you stay engaged and motivated over the long haul. If you don't believe me, look at history, where we have witnessed legendary leaders like Mahatma Gandhi, and Martin Luther King Jr. exhibit extraordinary dedication and perseverance through their compelling visions for the future. They were prepared to endure hardships and setbacks because their personal goals were important to them.

Moreover, SMART goals give employees a sense of purpose within the company, giving them autonomy and freedom to pursue their objectives the way they want, and autonomy is one of the most important factors in employee happiness studies.

Google has adopted this approach, permitting employees to devote 20% of their work hours towards personal projects. They know that employee autonomy results in greater efficiency and creativity, as employees are encouraged to accomplish goals they set for themselves.

What are SMART goals?

Let's revisit SMART goals, touched on earlier, as a definitive method of setting winning goals. SMART goals encapsulate the essence of effective goal setting:

They're specific, measurable, achievable, relevant, and time-bound - giving you clarity over what you want to accomplish and outlining how best to reach them. In the next section, we will look more closely at what is meant by each of these words.

How do you develop these SMART goals?

Are you ready to turn your aspirations into reality? In this section, I will help you find a goal-setting formula that works for you. I will suggest some prompts to make sure your goals are indeed specific, measurable, achievable, relevant, and time bound. You are going to define and write your goals down and don't worry if you don't get it 100% right on the first try, you can refine your goals until they are just right, but you must start somewhere.

I can hear some of you thinking about not writing down your goals and just keeping them 'in your head'. Don't fall into this common trap; write them down. Why? A Harvard Business study revealed that MBA graduates who wrote down their goals achieved significantly more success than those who didn't. In fact, the 3% who wrote down their goals earned up to 10 times more than the rest. Why not give yourself the best possible chance at success by taking this easy, simple extra step?

S - Get Specific

The secret here is to be as narrow as possible when you answer these prompts; this will lead you to create a goal that is specific enough to keep you motivated and on track.

Prompt 1 - What specific outcomes do you want to realize?

Example: I want to increase sales revenue by 20% within the next year.

Prompt 2 - What are your key details and specifics regarding this goal?

Example: I want to increase sales revenue by 20% within the next year by targeting new market segments and initiating an effective digital marketing campaign.

Prompt 3 - Who is involved in meeting this goal?

Example: My sales team, marketing department, and external consultants.

Prompt 4 - What resources or tools will they need to meet this goal?

Example: My company will allocate additional funding for marketing activities, training programs for the sales team, and accessing market research data.

By answering these prompts, you can formulate a precise goal that outlines what you wish to achieve, how it should be accomplished, who will be involved, and the necessary resources required. Being specific will give your goals clear direction and increase your chances of success.

M - Make it Measurable

Some goals can be measured simply by using things like timers or tracking software, while others will require more abstract ways to monitor progress.

Here are some prompts to help you make sure your goals are measurable:

Prompt 1 - How will I measure progress?

Example: I will note how many new leads I generate monthly and look at my website's analytics.

Prompt 2 - Do I have all the tools needed for accurate measurement?

Example: I've made sure that I have access to analytics software, CRM systems, or other tracking tools that will allow me to monitor key metrics related to achieving this goal.

Prompt 3 - How will I know I've reached my goal?

Example: I will set a reminder to check the analytics software every Monday morning to check progress towards my goal.

A - Make it Achievable

It's important to strike a good balance between ambitious and attainable when setting goals; this will help you avoid the extremes of goals that are impossible or too easy. Goals that are too ambitious present excessive challenges that lead to increased procrastination and usually frustration. At the same time, goals that are too easy may lead to a lack of inspiration and motivation. Realistic yet achievable goals should be designed to stretch and challenge you without overburdening you.

Use these prompts to find the right balance:

Prompt 1 - What resources and control do I have available to reach my goal?

Example answer: As a manager, I have sufficient budget and the authority to make any spending decisions designed to achieve sales growth.

Prompt 2 - How do I plan to implement my strategy?

Example answer: To reach a wide audience I will consider using digital multichannel marketing, with promotions through social media, adverts, and email.

Prompt 3 - How can I segment my goal into smaller, more manageable tasks?

Example Answer: I can segment my annual targets into specific quarterly and even monthly goals, incorporating strategies designed to achieve them, to track progress and implement changes early on and as needed.

Prompt 4 - Is my goal ambitious enough to keep me tested yet still engaged?

Example Answer: Requiring a 20% increase in sales is attainable with appropriate strategies based on market history. However, it requires techniques and effort from the sales force to get there, thus igniting exploration, new possibilities, and creativity.

Prompt 5 - What support would my team require to achieve their goals?

Example Answer: Over and above the teams' qualifications and experience, additional training in lead generation, negotiation, and customer relations can increase and fine-tune their skills.

R - Make sure the goal is Relevant

Ensure that goals are relevant to your current and long-term plans. A relevant goal aligns with your broader vision and fits seamlessly into the bigger picture, whether with personal aspirations or within a business setting.

To make your goal relevant, ask yourself the following questions:

Prompt 1 - Why is this goal important to me?

Example Answer: My sales growth goal directly contributes to the success and profitability of the businesses that I manage, as well as to my personal career goal of becoming a renowned leader in my industry.

Prompt 2 - Is this goal worthy of my time?

Example Answer: Absolutely. My time would be well-spent on this goal as it ties directly into the strategic objectives of my organization. By focusing on sales growth, I can contribute to its long-term financial security and success, ultimately benefitting both employees and stakeholders.

Prompt 3 - Is this the right time for this goal?

Example answer: Yes, now is an ideal time for us to pursue sales growth effectively. Market conditions are favourable, and we have all the resources and team support necessary for doing so effectively. Also, competitors are aggressively expanding their market shares, so it's crucial that we seize this opportunity quickly to remain ahead in our industry.

T - Ensure your goal is Time-bound

It is important to set time-bound goals to create a sense of urgency, accountability, and focus. Setting specific deadlines or target dates provides a roadmap for taking actions. But remember that however much time you give yourself, you will typically use it all as per Parkinson's Law![2]

Question 1 - When will I achieve the goal?

Example answer: I aim to achieve the goal of sales growth within the next fiscal year.

Question 2 - When will I carry out the activities that will bring me to my goal?

Example Answer: I will initiate marketing strategies and sales initiatives immediately. I will ensure all necessary subsequent actions are consistently taken throughout the year - such as running promotional campaigns, optimizing digital channels, and increasing performance of sales teams.

Question 3 - When can I expect the first outcomes

---

[2] Parkinson's Law states that work always expands to fill the time allotted for its completion.

Example Answer: My aim is to see tangible outcomes within the first quarter of this year. These could include increased lead generation, enhanced customer engagement and initial signs of sales growth.

Let's talk about action

> *Goals without action simply remain wishes*

Now that you have set SMART goals, it is time to put them in motion. Goals without action simply remain wishes - and only through taking deliberate and purposeful steps can your goals become tangible outcomes. In this section, we will explore practical steps to turn those wishes into reality.

Set a SMART action plan and stick to it

Once you've set your SMART goals, you must create an action plan, a road map if you will, that is aligned with your goals.

What if you have multiple SMART goals? Where do you start? This is where laser focus comes in. Pick the one goal that will move the needle the most and prioritize it. Dedicate at least 90 days to making substantial strides towards achieving it. Narrowing your focus prevents overwhelm and ensures that you and your team direct enough energy and attention toward that one goal, with the intent and promise of reaching it.

Next, you need to break your goal down into actionable steps with specific timelines for each one. Having clear milestones along the way enables you to keep track of progress and celebrate small wins on your way to the main goal. Make it part of your weekly routine to monitor progress.

Goal	Action Plan	Notes
Increase traffic to website 20% by the end of Q4	Establish a baseline to measure against	Use Google Analytics to record where we are currently (last 3 months)
	Run a promotional advert through social media channels	Directing visitors to the newsletter signup page on our website
	Send a newsletter to our existing customer base via email	Record the results in our CRM tool
	Monitor weekly and adjust ads according to visitor demographics	Use Google Analytics on our webpage to assess

Now, let's look at how you can effectively take action and drive behaviour to stick to the plan and meet the goals. Don't worry; it is much easier than you think.

Create Habits

When I first started my leadership journey, reaching big goals appeared as a mountain before me and felt like a lot of work. In my mind, I had to work hard to accomplish goals, and I also had to drive my team hard to meet deadlines and stick to the plan. This all changed when I learned about the power of habit.

Charles Duhigg, in his famous book "The Power of Habit," said: "Champions don't do extraordinary things. They do ordinary things but do them without thinking, too fast for the other team to react. They follow the habits they've learned." Imagine your entire organization learning habits that make following the plan and reaching your goals like second nature. Imagine every person showing up to work every day simply knowing what to do, they do it effortlessly, and the rewards come with ease. This is possible when you create winning habits within your organization.

Habits have the power to transform not only individuals but also entire organizations. Habits provide the basis upon which larger goals can be reached, and developing them requires consistency, structure, and accountability for success. Much like individuals need time and persistence before their actions become embedded as habits, similarly, organizations must prioritize important tasks, create regular routines, and incorporate these behaviours into their company procedures.

Tips to turn goal-oriented behaviours into enduring habits:

Prioritize important tasks as unchangeable appointments - Select tasks that support your goals and set aside specific times in your calendar for them. You should treat these activities with equal importance as formal meetings or events.

If, for example, customer satisfaction is one of your main goals, set aside enough time each day to respond promptly and effectively to customer inquiries.

Stick with a consistent schedule - Create and stick to an agenda that encompasses your most essential work activities and follow it closely. Doing this creates predictability while helping to ensure tasks get accomplished without you feeling overwhelmed.

For example, as a team leader, you should prioritize setting regular meetings with team members to provide updates, address challenges and monitor progress.

Rethink your behaviour as part of who you are - To increase self-esteem and motivation, adopt habits that lead to professional success; doing this raises both self-esteem and motivation, encouraging long-term behaviour change.

For instance, if being on time for work will help build credibility and set an example for team members, then consistent punctuality will not only benefit you professionally but will also give you a sense of personal accomplishment.

Utilize habit stacking - This technique enables you to continually learn and evolve by adding positive new habits onto existing ones. Start by choosing habits that give you a solid base, then expand on those with new ones aligning with professional growth and development goals.

If, for example, reviewing industry news during morning coffee breaks has become part of your routine, try setting aside a specific time each week for learning new skills or enrolling in relevant online courses.

Adopting these strategies and integrating them into your workplace routine develops powerful habits that contribute to your success, helping both you and your organization to reach SMART goals quicker.

Take concrete steps to ensure you make it happen

Hold yourself accountable

To reach your goals, you must hold yourself accountable for the actions that you need to take. Without accountability and ownership, procrastination can easily sneak in, and you may struggle to get important things done. Accountability forces you to follow through and stay motivated. How do you hold yourself accountable? Sharing your goals with others and asking them to hold you accountable reduces procrastination while strengthening your sense of ownership and responsibility. You could find an accountability partner, like a mentor or coach, to give you feedback, and guidance, and troubleshoot with when you start to veer off the track. Remember to write down your plans and commitments for that extra accountability.

Track your progress

Imagine how disheartening it would be NOT to see the progress bar when backing up precious photos. You would be unsure if it was working or not. With a visible

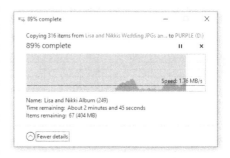

progress bar you can better plan your time and get on with other tasks if it looks like it will take a while. It's exactly the same in business.

Tracking progress towards our objectives is essential. Goals define your desired achievements, while OKRs (Objectives and Key Results) provide evidence of progress toward these objectives. To stay on the right path, track key results with regular progress reviews and schedule check points as milestones are reached - this will ensure you stay engaged and prevent you from micromanaging your team.

Update your goals as needed

Goals are not set in stone; you must remain flexible and reevaluate your goals from time to time to accommodate life changes and ever-evolving circumstances. On a monthly or quarterly basis, revisit your goals to assess whether they are still relevant and aligned with your values.

Envisioning your goals as flexible, living things will help you feel less intimidated by the entire goal-setting exercise, as you will realize that they are not permanent. If you get it wrong (for example, you choose a goal that is not 100% in alignment with your values), you get a chance to amend or change the goal.

There is also a constant influx of unexpected outside influences, take Covid or Brexit for example, that can hamper any business and cause you to adjust and re-adjust your goals accordingly.

Stop self-sabotaging behaviour in its tracks

I have often found myself needing to work on goal setting throughout my life, and the excuses I would make were endless; one of the most persistent was that I believed that my goals were abstract and did not fit in with the framework because they were not like the ones in previous examples I had seen. As time went on, I discovered that most, if not all, of the limiting thoughts I had about creating goals were nothing more than just that, limiting beliefs.

Limiting belief: I don't know what term to set goals for
Goals can be long, medium, or short-term. They do not have to be 40-year, 3-year, or 10-year goals. You can have anything from a daily goal to a 50, 60, or 70-year goal. There are no rules here, and the framework works for all kinds of goals.

Limiting belief: I don't know how often to set goals
The frequency of goal setting depends on the type of goal, with professional goals typically set annually or quarterly with regular reviews, while personal goals should be considered more frequently, with monthly check-ins for progress assessment. Also, you can't get it wrong; doing it at your pace is much, much better than not doing it at all.

Limiting belief: I don't know what's "Realistic" anymore
With the world changing at ever increasing speeds, it is unsurprising that this belief exists. However, by looking at your

previous goals, and comparing them against your current situation, it should be possible to decide if a goal is realistic or not. Ask yourself if any circumstances have changed? Any relevant new laws or cumbersome regulations? Have staff received further training that might change the speed or efficiency of reaching your goals?

Apply the lessons from reaching past goals to future endeavours and adapt accordingly. Remember that it's not just about the destination itself; pay attention to both the journey and the quality of the process - reflect upon the progress the team has made, recognize milestones as you reach them, and learn from any setbacks that you experience along the way.

As a leader, it's vital that you remain present and accessible to your team. Be there when they need guidance, support, or encouragement as they work toward their goals and offer assistance when needed.

Be open to constructive criticism and welcome feedback from team members as a valuable source of insight, as their perspectives can help refine your approach. By actively seeking their opinions, you will create an atmosphere of trust and collaboration.

Finally, take time to enjoy the process of setting and achieving SMART goals for your team. Establish a culture of goal setting and achievement; this has a tremendous impact on morale and team success; promote a culture that values personal development while supporting team members as they celebrate milestones together.

By following these principles, not only will you become an effective manager who guides your team toward success but also an inspirational leader who creates an enjoyable work environment.

Now that we have covered the crucial steps of goal setting, planning, and acting, it is time to shift our focus to another vital aspect of effective leadership, namely effective decision-making.

Decision making

The importance of great decision making

One crucial aspect often gets overlooked: decision-making. Yes, the ability to make choices and take responsibility for them lies at the heart of effective leadership. It's time to shift the focus from merely having a laundry list of desirable leadership traits to putting your leadership skills into action.

Remember the Ben Horowitz quote from chapter 2?

"Hard things are hard because there are no easy answers or recipes. They are hard because your emotions are at odds with your logic. They are hard because you don't know the answer, and you cannot ask for help without showing weakness."

This is the hard part of leadership, and this is also when true leaders shine. In times like these, the hard times, true leaders are prepared to make solid decisions and to continue when it feels unsafe to turn either way.

By making choices and decisions, especially when it is not easy, you can shape the direction and outcome of your team's efforts. However, this is where many leaders fail because they are too afraid of both failure and criticism.

To truly otep into your loadorchip potential, you must conquer your fear of decision-making; this means you cannot hide behind indecision or let circumstances dictate the path forward. You must take charge and make choices that align with your vision and goals. Remember, logic alone cannot always guide you towards the best option - sometimes, it takes courage to put "your neck on the line" and trust your instincts.

Why does it matter? Why can't I just "go with the flow?"

You will improve workplace productivity - Effective decision-making saves time and propels work projects forward, increasing employee productivity. Clear decisions help employees focus on tasks.

You will be decisive in emergency situations - Leaders sometimes need to make quick, impactful decisions during emergencies to minimize damage and optimize benefits. Being able to effectively assess organizational needs and decide the best course of action ensures business continuity and support for employees.

You will establish trust with employees - Thoughtful decision-making demonstrates that managers value their employees' work and have their best interests in mind. By evaluating, analysing, and explaining decisions, leaders can build trust and encourage open communication with their teams.

You will reduce conflict - The decision-making process reduces conflict and minimises misunderstandings, by setting clear expectations for employees.

How is your decision-making?

Take a moment to assess your current leadership abilities in the realm of decision-making. Ask yourself these three important questions, reflect on your answers, and evaluate if you need to do some work on your decision-making abilities:

- Have you avoided making leading decisions in the past four weeks?
- Have you made leading decisions in the past four weeks?
- Would your team agree that you make brave leading decisions?

Top decision-makers excel in the following skills:

The ability to do research - Making informed decisions is derived from collecting and internalizing enough information to be able to apply it to your specific situation. For example, if you have a product that you need to market, you would start by doing research to determine the best possible platform to market it on, including looking at different social media platforms, who their audience is, and what their community standards are to choose the most effective one.

Creative thinking - Creativity plays an invaluable role in decision-making. Employing this type of thinking breaks away from conventional approaches and explores more innovative solutions, allowing you to think outside the box, consider multiple possibilities, challenge established norms, and generate original ideas that tap into diverse perspectives.

Critical thinking - By carefully considering your alternatives, assessing outcomes, and aligning choices with organizational goals, critical thinking will help you make sound choices. As you hone this skill, you learn to evaluate risks, challenge assumptions, and select the best path toward success.

Time management - During the decision-making process, it is vital to manage your time carefully. You want to take enough time to evaluate options and gather information. Yet, you also want to make sure you are making the decision promptly, avoiding over-analysing and causing 'analysis paralysis' to the point where you take no decision or action at all.

Emotional intelligence - We have already discussed emotional intelligence, and decision-making is one of the places in your leadership journey where this skill will be most helpful. Become aware of your emotions; how do you feel about the potential outcomes? How are you reacting to specific solutions? Do your best to observe and control your emotions during the decision-making process so that you make decisions from a rational place.

Decision-making options

A question you may be asking yourself is whether you should make decisions on your own, get input from others or even decide by group consensus.

Single Person Decides: In this case, based on your expertise, experience and authority, you may choose to make a decision without seeking input from others.

Group Decides by Consensus: With open group discussions you can encourage your team to reach a consensus on a change. For example, you may gather input from team members on whether to switch to a new software package or upgrade your existing system.

Group Decides by Voting: In situations where consensus is difficult to achieve, you may even facilitate a voting process to decide. For instance, as a department head, you may call for a vote among team members to determine the new dress code policy. The option with the majority vote becomes the chosen policy.

Decision-making styles

As a leader, you must assess the circumstances and choose the appropriate decision-maker style based on factors such as urgency, the expertise required, and the level of involvement desired by team members.

There are four primary decision-making styles characterized by task or social focus and a high or low tolerance for ambiguity. Styles with a high tolerance for ambiguity can handle uncertain variables in reaching a conclusion, while those with a low tolerance seek clarity in decision-making.

By recognizing your style and being aware of others' styles, you can make informed choices that align with your career goals and suit specific situations.

1. The **directive decision-making style** uses quick, decisive thinking to come to a solution. A directive decision-maker has a low tolerance for vague or ambiguous ideas. They're focused on the task and will use their own knowledge and judgment to come to a conclusion with selective input from others.

    Example: As a project manager, you need to decide whether to allocate additional resources to meet a tight deadline. After assessing the project's progress and considering the potential impact on other tasks, you make a quick decision to reallocate resources from another project to ensure timely completion.

2. **Analytical decision-makers** carefully analyse data to come up with a solution. They're adaptable thinkers. They will invest time to glean information to form a conclusion. These decision-makers are task-oriented but have a high tolerance for ambiguity.

    Example: As a sales manager, you are tasked with choosing the most effective pricing strategy for a new product launch. You gather data on market trends, competitor pricing, and customer preferences. After carefully analysing the information, you decide on a pricing structure that maximizes profitability and rewards loyalty.

3. Those who make decisions with a **conceptual style** are big-picture thinkers who are willing to take risks. They evaluate different options and possibilities with a high tolerance for ambiguity. They're social-oriented and take the time to consider big ideas and creative solutions.

    Example: As the CEO of a tech startup, you want to explore new business opportunities. You brainstorm ideas with your team and envision the potential outcomes and market impact. After evaluating the risks and rewards, you make a bold decision to invest in developing a cutting-edge product that has the potential to revolutionize the industry.

4. A **behavioural style of decision-making** focuses on relationships more than the task. It evaluates the feelings of others as part of their decision-making process. Behaviour decision-makers have a low tolerance for ambiguity and a social focus as they evaluate solutions.

    Example: As a team leader, you need to resolve a conflict among team members regarding the division of tasks. You hold a group discussion, actively listening to everyone's perspectives and concerns. Considering the team's dynamics and individual strengths, you facilitate a consensus-based decision, ensuring everyone feels heard and involved in the process.

A step-by-step guide for Decision-Making

Let's look at a simple step-by-step guide to help you become a master at making top-quality decisions for your life and your business.

Step 1: Identify the challenge - Take time to discover the nature of the issue and find out what circumstances led to the situation in the first place.

Step 2: Decide who will decide - Identify who will make decisions based on factors such as expertise, time availability, and the importance of decisions. Make decisions at the lowest level possible.

If the decision is to be made by a group, you must create an environment where everyone will feel free to express their thoughts, encouraging open communication and active participation.

Step 3: Come up with solutions - Once you have a better understanding of the issue, you can now create possible solutions. Having more than one potential solution is a good idea because it opens the possibility of discovering innovative and creative approaches that may not be immediately apparent.

Step 4: Weigh up your options - Carefully look at the advantages and disadvantages of each option and explore alternative solutions if you need to.

Step 5: Make a choice - Once you have looked at the challenge, come up with several possible solutions, and weighed them up against one another, it is time to decide.

In my life, I have a policy of trusting my decision-making, so once I have made a decision, I do not second guess myself; I trust that I did the best I could with the information I had at the time, and I move on to the next order of business. This helps prevent me from overthinking and ruminating.

Step 6: Communicate - Now, it is time to let others know about the decision and explain how it might influence them. If there are disagreements about your decision, this is also the time to stand firm in explaining your process. This will garner the support of your team when they see that you have confidence in your decision-making process and abilities.

Hiding decisions or unveiling them suddenly only causes unnecessary speculation and anxiety, thus damaging trust between employees. Leaders should prioritize clarity and transparency, even when complete information isn't yet available, to prevent negativity from filling any void of uncertainty that might exist.

Be clear and concise. Effective decision-making goes beyond simply choosing one option over another - it requires providing thorough explanations and answering any pertinent questions raised about any decision that has been made. Failing to adequately explain factors leading to a specific action and potential ramifications damages trust between leaders and their followers. Leaders should communicate openly, providing stakeholders with all the required information for them to comprehend and accept a decision being made.

Step 7: Follow Through - Ensure that the decision is effectively executed and implemented by assigning responsibilities to your team members, creating timelines, and ensuring that your team has the necessary support and resources to drive the decision to successful conclusion.

Deciding not to decide

I have stressed the importance of making informed decisions; however, sometimes, deferring or postponing making one may be beneficial. Why is that?

As important as it is to make timely decisions and solicit input from your group, being seen as impulsive rather than decisive can have devastating effects on team dynamics. Acting quickly to make a decision without gathering all the necessary information or providing your team a chance to express themselves can create dissatisfaction or resistance among teammates.

Sometimes the wisest course of action is delaying making an immediate decision. A careful assessment may reveal it is more prudent to wait for additional data or allow teammates time to calm down after an animated debate before deciding.

Let's look at an example: Assume a project team is discussing different marketing strategies for launching a new product and is divided on which approach is the best fit, each side having strong arguments for their choice. Instead of making a snap decision right away, their leader decides to hold another meeting to gather more data and allow reflection on all presented arguments. This approach ensures all perspectives are taken into consideration and increases chances for making informed and inclusive decisions.

Problem-led leadership

In my pursuit of understanding leadership styles that shape the world, I discovered one additional, distinct type of leadership, namely problem-led leadership, and it is a very different approach that certainly defies convention. Problem-led leaders don't seek personal followership; instead, they ignite enthusiasm by presenting compelling problems in need of innovative solutions.

They reluctantly assume leadership roles, but their focus is on driving progress, not on personal charisma or status. Problem-led leadership is characterized by fluidity, with individuals stepping up and again stepping aside as the project demands.

Deep expertise and the ability to assemble talented teams form the foundation of this emerging style of leadership. While discomfort with the term "leadership" persists, these individuals lead by solving problems and inspiring others to do the same. This is becoming a global movement where passionate individuals tackle challenges, energize teams, and achieve breakthrough results.

Let's look at problem-solving a little more closely to get a better understanding of this leadership style.

What is problem-solving?

Problem-solving is a specific method of thinking, and it is considered by many to be the most complex of all intellectual functions. It is defined as a higher-order cognitive skill, and it is used when one doesn't know how to go from your current state to a goal or ideal state.

Problem-solving is an art, and the good news is that with practice, you can get better at it. Planning and structuring are two essential components of problem-solving, while good judgment and an element of good luck will help make your problem-solving more successful.

Why is problem-solving important?

Problem-solving is essential in both meeting immediate challenges and preventing future ones.
In personal relationships, effective problem-solving can improve intimacy and trust.

As a leader, problem-solving capabilities allow you to remain composed under pressure, assess situations more thoroughly, make accurate predictions, and make decisions that have positive outcomes.

Poor problem-solving skills, (leading to issues not being detected, being ignored or poorly addressed), can have devastating repercussions for interpersonal relationships and businesses alike.

Recognizing the root causes behind problems rather than only treating surface symptoms is an integral component of problem-solving; when dealing with customer complaints, for instance, it's key to establish their source in order to address and eliminate them effectively.

A Step-By-Step Guide for Problem-Solving

Problem-solving, by its very nature, can seem daunting because, by the time you come to implement these skills, there is something else that needs fixing. It may be urgent, or it may be a looming problem that you can take some time on. Either way, you need a clear structure or framework to help guide you through careful and effective problem-solving.

Similar to decision-making, here is your seven-step guide for effective problem-solving;

Step 1 - Identify and Define the Problem: Take time to fully understand and characterize the scope and nature of the issue at hand. Be specific in identifying when and how this should be resolved.

Step 2 - Analyse the Problem: Evaluate its effect on your business overall and gather information regarding who, what, when, where, why, and how the problem occurred to pinpoint its root cause and find permanent solutions.

Step 3 – Use the Data: Collect and assess relevant data to gain a fact-based understanding of your problem and its solution. Interpreting data will help identify specific issues and support resolution strategies.

Step 4 - Communicate: To effectively relay the problem and present solutions to key stakeholders, develop strong communication skills. Encourage honest feedback and diverse perspectives while remaining transparent throughout.

Step 5 - Be Adaptable: Resist being averse to change or risk-taking, examine beyond apparent details, and consider taking risks for innovative approaches. Make an effort to include contributions from all team members as you explore new perspectives.

Step 6 - Create Solutions: Brainstorm and choose several fully developed options from amongst them; present only those you think would work best for stakeholders or clients for decision-making purposes, considering time, cost, and technology requirements when selecting solutions.

Step 7 - Learn from Mistakes: View mistakes as opportunities for growth and learning, reflect upon your problem-solving approach and process, and make modifications that will enable greater efficiency, creativity, and speed in future endeavours.

* * *

Goal setting, inspiring action, decision-making, and problem-solving all require communication, and as such it is a fundamental and extremely important quality in leadership. If there's one set of skills that all others rely on, it's communication. So, let's take a deeper look...

Chapter 9 - Talk Like a Leader

"Speech is one symptom of Affection
And Silence one—
The perfectest communication
Is heard of none—"

- Emily Dickinson,
Speech Is One Symptom of Affection

Human connection is the baseline of our existence. Without it, we are rudderless, and all our efforts become void of meaning. So how does that affect us as leaders? Truthfully, this connection is the penultimate goal of any great leader, and to achieve it, you will need to master the art of **creating a rapport** with your team, through both **effective communication** and **active listening**. Only through successfully navigating these skills will you be able to inspire, to connect, and to nurture those all-important relationships.

The value of effective communication between leaders and their team has been proven to increase productivity, improve employee satisfaction, encourage higher rates of engagement, reduce absenteeism, decrease turnover rates, improve morale, enhance customer service quality, and even promote safety, health, and general well-being. So, despite this long list of benefits, why is it that leaders still struggle to get it right?

Sadly, it is due to the three very common communication killers, which are;

1) Not listening
2) Interrupting
3) Multi-Tasking

Have you ever spoken to someone and felt frustrated by the fact that they simply weren't "getting it" - that even though they were clearly *hearing* you and responding to you, they just weren't listening? Well, that is exactly what I mean when I talk about communication killers.

The fact is that listening may seem like a simple skill but the urge to speed things along, to check your phone during a long meeting or zoom call, or even to space out a little because you are stressed out about a project at work, is far too tempting and altogether common. As a leader, the onus is on you to ask empowering questions, to listen closely without spoon-feeding simple answers, and to guide your team to explore solutions for themselves.

Since all three of the communication killers I discussed above are related to listening, the very first skill we will work on is that of **Active Listening**. This skill is perhaps one of the most important you will ever learn to master and can be extremely transformative when done right. We will look at practical advice for being present, speaking authentically, and forming deep connections.

The second skill we will look at is **Effective Communication**. Here, we will examine conviction, clarity, and adaptability. I will share some simple tools that you will be able to use to encourage understanding, inspire those around you, and speak as a leader would speak.

The third and final skill we will work on in this chapter is that of **Building Rapport**. We need to be able to create harmonious relationships, implement empathy, and be genuinely present. Throughout this chapter, we will be looking deeper into human connection and communication through body language, micro expressions, and shared energy.

Active Listening

What is active listening?

As we alluded to earlier, there is a difference between hearing and listening. Hearing is simply the biological act of receiving and responding to the stimulus of sound. Listening is more complicated, requires concentration and mental effort, and is an essential skill for good leaders to learn. True listening is based on fully engaging with the speaker, both verbally and nonverbally, and it forms the foundation on which to build trust, understanding, and strengthened relationships.

It's important that when we listen, we do so by giving the other person our full attention instead of simply thinking of how we are going to respond or worse, waiting for a gap in their chatter to leap in and fill the space with our own words.
Focus on what the speaker is saying, how they are saying it, and the meaning of the interaction or what it is that they are trying to impart to you or request from you.

Active listening allows us to home in on the real message behind the conversation by identifying non-verbal cues and critically assessing the information at hand. It allows us to increase connection by showing genuine interest, prioritizing others, and creating a shared understanding.

Ever been party to a conversation where someone is talking *at* you instead of *to* you? This type of monologue-based communication is quite common to the authoritarian leadership style and can stifle your ability to engage with your team and sustain an open dialogue.

Take Lisa for example, Lisa is a newly appointed manager and is struggling with the reality of being promoted into a leadership role. She is excited about her position but struggles to lead confidently, succumbing to the effects of IS. At times, she feels a bit overwhelmed and desperately wants to connect better with her team.

One afternoon, a distressed colleague, who also happened to be a friend, asked her out of frustration (or perhaps even desperation) to put her phone down while she was speaking. It was a real "A-ha!" moment that made Lisa realize that she had been neglecting the people she was meant to be connecting with. Lisa had been so overwhelmed that she would lose herself in her work and would barely even lift her head when someone spoke to her, simply giving a logical response without real connection. If it had not been for that moment, she may have gone years without realizing her mistake, and she decided that day to make a change.

In the next weekly meeting, Lisa noticed that a team member, Sarah, seemed reluctant to express herself. She took action by employing active listening techniques (more about this later), consciously giving Sarah her full attention while maintaining eye contact and leaning in with genuine interest.

Lisa noticed that Sarah was passionate but also accompanied by a certain amount of anxiety when she spoke for the first time. Acknowledging this with an empathetic nod instead of interrupting or rejecting Sarah's ideas, Lisa listened actively, allowing Sarah's ideas to flow freely, creating an environment where Sarah felt valued, supported, and heard.

Once the meeting was over, Sarah approached Lisa and thanked her for allowing her to share her ideas without being judged or interrupted. Lisa's attentive listening not only had an immediate positive effect on Sarah, but it also created a stronger working relationship between them. This experience made Lisa understand the significance of active listening. She realized that she could easily build trust and empower her team members, just by making this one change.

Guidelines for effective listening:

Lisa's story shows us that active listening can be quite powerful and is crucial to becoming a stronger leader. It is often overlooked, many of us equate communication with speaking, but when done right, it has a massive impact. It can be challenging at times to overcome the barriers of communication. One such barrier is the tendency for your mind to wander off after just a few sentences or to become distracted. This is caused by the fact that your brain processes information much faster than the average speech rate. This also means that the human brain is predisposed to 'tune out' and that it requires real effort to listen actively.

Remember that your body language gives you away when you are not truly listening and that a lack of attention or interest cannot be hidden. Staying present, embracing active listening, and being aware of your body language during conversations, enhances your ability to listen with respect and engagement.

Here are some helpful techniques to become better at active listening:

Be present - Give the speaker your undivided attention. Remove distractions and show genuine interest in what they have to say. Be conscious of your body language; nodding or using affirmative and appropriate gestures shows engagement.

I once had a manager who, while he was a very important and busy man, would close his laptop and refuse to take phone calls while anyone was consulting him in his office. The first time I experienced this, I was amazed at the attention he gave me, a mere junior in the company. I have respected him immensely since that day and see him as one of the greatest leaders I have ever encountered because of that single act of active listening.

Make eye contact: A natural but intentional amount of eye contact shows that you are paying attention to everything that the other person says. Practice makes perfect when it comes to eye contact; start with a good amount of looking directly at a person and tone it down if you pick up on subtle clues of discomfort that you might be doing it too much. It will only take a short while to figure out the right balance for a good conversation.

Smile: As with eye contact, you will need to experiment with smiling. You should aim to find the right balance within the conversation and look for an appropriate time to smile. This naturally depends on the person, the topic, and the setting. Use your intuition and know why you are smiling. A genuine smile goes a long way; you don't need to fake it.

Paraphrase and rephrase - After hearing someone share their thoughts, summarize what was said to ensure that you understand what they are trying to communicate to you, then paraphrase the key points to show that you're actively listening. This also helps to clear up any misunderstandings.

Remember that this is not just an act of reflecting the information back to the person you are listening to. Active listening means that you need to understand the essence of what is being said. If you are thinking about your response while they are speaking, you may be able to recite words back to them, but you won't be able to grasp the real meaning of the interaction. Trust me when I tell you that the other person will know the difference.

Ask open-ended questions - Invite further discussion by asking open-ended questions. Encourage the person speaking to expand on their ideas, give more details, and express their emotions freely. Avoid close-ended enquiries that require simple yes/no answers. For example, instead of asking someone: "Do you agree with our marketing strategy proposal?" (a close-ended question), you can ask: "So, what do you think of the new marketing strategy we have proposed?" and follow up with: "How do you think it aligns with our overall strategy?". You can see how the first question invites only a "yes" or "no" answer, while the second approach invites a conversation.

Some more examples of good open-ended questions include:

- Can you tell me more about that idea?
- How do you think we could make this work?
- What alternative solutions could we consider here?

Practice empathy - The ability to put yourself in someone else's shoes is an essential facet of active listening. When you work on your ability to understand something from someone else's perspective, it allows you to acknowledge their emotions and validate their experiences. This also enables you to respond with kindness and compassion.

Allow space for emotions - Sharing sensitive information or discussing personal topics can often evoke strong emotional responses. Make sure to reiterate that it's normal to feel these emotions and that it is important to express them. It may be helpful to have a box of Kleenex on your desk for particularly intense moments. It can be surprisingly comforting to be handed a tissue when you are overwhelmed; when done in a kind and gentle way, it becomes like a wordless way to allow space for emotion and humanity. Respectfully give the person a moment to compose themselves. This simple act of kindness will forge strong relationships at work and create trust in your team.

Avoid judgment: Creating a non-judgemental environment encourages people to feel more comfortable and will allow them to share their thoughts more freely. Avoid jumping to conclusions and forming opinions too early. You may be surprised how much you can learn from others when you step away from biases or previously adopted frameworks.

Active silence: Silence can be as effective as a worded response. It encourages the person to share more and provides an opportunity for them to explore their sentiment in a way that they may not have been able to if they were interrupted. When you are the one person that gives others that extra bit of space to speak, you become trusted with their thoughts and leave a lasting impression. People remember the way you make them *feel*, and this is an easy way to make the speaker feel important and heard.

Maintain proper posture: Lean forward slightly or sideways when sitting to show the other person that you are fully engaged and listening to them. Avoid slouching back, which can signal disinterest. Keep an open posture; crossing your arms or your legs will make you appear stand-offish and subconsciously make the other person more guarded and less likely to communicate openly.

Practice mirroring: When listening actively to another person, you should experiment with mirroring their facial expressions to signal understanding, trust, and being in sync. Be careful, though, not to go overboard and copy their every move like a mime artist. That might make them think you're not paying attention and that you've read Dale Carnegies'

"How to Win Friends and Influence People" one too many times. Remember, the magic lies in the subtlety.

Minimize distractions: Avoid fidgeting, checking the time, or engaging in distracting behaviours such as doodling or playing with your hair. When you are genuinely actively listening and constantly refocusing your attention on the conversation (this may not come naturally in the beginning), you won't have the urge to keep yourself busy with these minor distractions. If you do start fidgeting, for example, take it as a sign that you are losing focus and intentionally reconnect with the conversation.

Don't rush - Take your time; before you move on to a new topic, make sure the current one is wrapped up nicely. This can be as simple as taking a long breath, allowing for the messages to land, and asking the other person if they've got anything else to say. This gives your counterpart a chance to speak their mind and to tie up any loose ends. This way, when the conversation naturally comes to an end, you can smoothly transition to a new topic without leaving the other person feeling ignored or annoyed. Remember, when in doubt, just ask! No need to play mind-reader or rely on guesswork.

In the simplest terms, active listening shows respect and understanding. It is the easiest way to create an environment where people feel safe to express their ideas or concerns. Please remember that active listening requires dedication and practice to become truly effective.

Listening Remotely

The reality of remote-based working and online meetings has left many of us at a loss when it comes to creating trust and building connections. How can we engage with people when we cannot relate to them in person? To this end, I have added some extra tips about active listening in a world of endless Zoom meetings. These extra insights will prove worthwhile to explore, as active listening remains invaluable even when we are working remotely.

My main piece of advice here is that instead of looking at platforms such as Slack or Zoom as the enemy, you should think about how you can use them more effectively and adapt your active listening techniques specifically for remote communication.

Adopt the following practices to improve remote interactions:

- Maintain eye contact when speaking, even when done on camera, to show engagement and respect. Nod, smile, and demonstrate attentive listening for maximum impact.
- Make note-taking visible during meetings. Share the fact that you will be taking notes early in the meeting to hold yourself accountable and to prepare your counterparts.
- Take some time before video calls to clear your mind. Make an intentional effort to prepare yourself for active listening. Set expectations by communicating the purpose of each call in advance, enabling efficient and productive dialogues.
- Recognize the value of engaging in small talk to establish a rapport and encourage approachability. Initiate conversations that demonstrate a genuine interest in what the other person is discussing, creating an informal yet comfortable atmosphere.

Active listening should extend to messaging platforms like Slack and Teams. Acknowledging messages by responding in a timely fashion, sharing emoji reactions, or even a simple acknowledgment that you have read the message will ensure that people feel heard and valued.

Effective Communication

What is Effective Communication?

Let's start by asking: What is effective communication, and what does it look like?

Effective communication is the ability to exchange ideas and information in a way that can be readily received and understood.
It requires clarity and purpose and, when done properly, will leave everyone feeling satisfied with the interaction. It comes down to communicating with conviction, respect, and vision in a way that welcomes feedback and forward-thinking.

Effective communication relies both on what your message is and how you deliver it. Make sure you take the time to think about the context of what you are saying and who you are saying it to before you speak. Language choice, volume, tone, and even body language are all extremely important factors in effective communication.

Make sure you 'think before you speak' about the best way to encourage understanding, buy-in for your ideas, and impart the crux of your message with the biggest impact.

An example of Effective Communication in Action

Let's travel back in time and look at Margaret Thatcher, who was commonly referred to as "The Iron Lady," serving as Britain's Prime Minister from 1979-1990. Thatcher left a mark on history thanks to her powerful leadership style. Her communication techniques were extremely effective, and she was considered by many a force to be reckoned with.

Thatcher faced numerous challenges during her term as Prime Minister, including economic turmoil, political opposition, and social unrest. Yet her ability to communicate clearly, sometimes forcefully, and always persuasively was essential in moulding her leadership style and reaching her goals.

One iconic example of Thatcher's ability to communicate effectively was her speech at the 1984 Conservative Party Conference, also known as the "Sermon on the Mound." During a time of increasing criticism and opposition to her policies and values, Thatcher chose to speak passionately in defence of her position. She managed not only to make her point heard with clarity, but she was also able to earn the support of her audience. It was a remarkable display of effective communication at work.

Everyone was glued to the edge of their seats. Her demeanour held their attention, and her message resonated with different people from various walks of life. Thatcher recognized the significance of nonverbal communication. She used body language, facial expression, and tone of voice to strengthen her messages and build trust. Through attentive eye contact, appropriate gestures, and unwavering confidence, she projected authenticity and instilled trust in her leadership. Her speeches provided a clear vision, winning the confidence of her followers and rallying the party behind her leadership. Thatcher managed to navigate turbulent times without losing her authority as an effective leader.

The truth of this success is even more impressive when you consider that Thatcher was not a natural communicator. To her credit, she recognized the importance of effective communication in her role as a leader and sought guidance and training from Gordon Reece, an advisor who played a significant role in refining her communication skills and helping her develop her unique style.

Isn't it encouraging and empowering to realize that even an iconic communicator like Margaret Thatcher still had to learn to communicate and managed to get so good at it that she led a nation?

How to Enhance Effective Communication as a Leader

As we have seen above, even the greatest leaders needed to learn these skills, with the help of mentors and advisors. You may not currently be the strongest communicator, but with some time and practice, you can be as effective and impactful as the great leaders of our times.

As well as active listening, here are the main focus areas for effective communication:

Vocal production: Your voice reveals volumes about you. Your tone and word choice gives insight into your emotional state. A wavering voice could indicate low self-esteem, while soft-spoken speech can indicate shyness; conversely, someone with confidence would display a commanding voice with clear speech patterns. Consider investing in your vocal ability if you have voice habits that are hindering your communication.

Breath: Understanding the relationship between breath and voice enables you to harness it more effectively. Breath will dictate pacing, volume, and even emotional expression. Taking slow, deep breaths will allow for better vocal control while providing a steady supply of air that supports it.

Nonverbal communication: Be conscious of your body language, facial expressions, and tone of voice. Maintain eye contact, when possible, use appropriate gestures, and exude confidence when speaking aloud. Remember, to gain the trust of your team, your nonverbal and verbal communication needs to be in sync.

Clarity and conciseness: Speak plainly when communicating your ideas, avoid using complex language or jargon, and avoid saying too much and overwhelming people. Keep to the point with direct language so everyone can easily understand your message.

Adaptability: Tailor your communication style to meet the needs of your team. Think about the person you are talking to and how they best receive feedback. Some individuals respond best to data-driven arguments, while others prefer storytelling and anecdotes as motivational tools. Being flexible ensures effective communication across the board.

Use tact: You do need to be honest to be an effective communicator, but that does not mean you need to be brutal. Exercising control and caution when choosing your words is extremely important. That is why it is essential to prepare for important discussions where you know that you will have to address sensitive issues.

Be strategic with your words: Building on the last point, become strategic with your words. Do your research and, again, prepare. It will benefit you greatly to always frame messages in the most appealing light while remaining honest.

Prepare in advance: Don't fall into the trap of "winging it." Always plan out important conversations or messages, preferably write them down. Anticipate potential questions or challenges and prepare responses to ensure a confident reply.

Remember to add emotion: Emotion can drive action, which is why it is important not to fall into the trap of merely focusing on logical facts. You are speaking to a human being, after all, and it is important to balance emotion and logic to create a genuine connection.

Be honest: To build trust you must ensure that what you say matches what you do and what your body language says.

Look for subtext: When you really listen and focus on the other person, you will learn to see their words in perspective and read much more into their communication than only the words they say. 'Reading between the lines' will mean that you will be able to relate to the person you are communicating with and show them that you are invested in the conversation.

Use visual aids: Incorporate visuals, such as slides or diagrams, to enhance understanding and engagement. Some people are more visual than others, so while you may be tempted to speak from your knowledge and gut, others who are more visually inclined will be able to follow you much better with visual aids.

Clarify: Encourage questions and provide clarification to ensure that everyone is on the same page. If people are not free to challenge and respond, communication becomes incomplete and ineffective.

Ask for feedback: Don't assume that people received your message in the way that you intended for it to be heard. Rather, check in with them, ask concept-checking questions, and ask what they took from your message. If the message wasn't understood the right way, then try again.

Shorten sentences: short sentences are easier to process and understand and create a sense of urgency, which inspires action.

Simple words: Simpler words are easier to understand, they make it easy for your team to absorb and process your message.

Communicate with a servant's heart: Contribute better by giving more than you take. Showing empathy and care in your communication will become easier as the trust within your team grows.

Open your mind to opposing views: Take the time to understand and be willing to change your mind when you learn new information that brings you new insights.

Understand your subject matter: Know what you are talking about, or you will not be respected or given the time of day in conversations.

Be agile: Be flexible and willing to change your message if needed. Have a contingency plan for crucial conversations that are not going well.

By developing effective communication skills, you will be better equipped to articulate your vision, inspire your team, and navigate challenging situations with finesse. Take inspiration from these suggestions and make the lessons and tips in this section your own.

Building Rapport

What does it mean to build rapport?

Now for the real test of great leadership: building rapport. Establishing rapport with your team is an integral part of good communication and can be an absolute game-changer when done right.

In some cases, it will happen naturally and seemingly instantaneously. You'll recognize this when someone instantly "clicks" or they "just get along." The good news is that you can also nurture this type of connection intentionally. It requires the forging of relationships, earning trust, and developing a harmonious environment.

Building rapport in business offers many advantages. By nurturing strong relationships, your employees will become more engaged and motivated, leading to higher productivity. Building rapport also creates an open atmosphere where employees feel free to provide feedback, allowing continuous development and improvement. It earns your team's loyalty, which is invaluable to long-term success. It is also a cost-effective strategy to motivate team members, surpassing monetary bonuses.

Let's look at my favourite example of someone who knows how to effectively build rapport: Michelle Obama. Michelle is an extraordinary individual with remarkable interpersonal skills that enable her to connect with people deeply. From her tenure as First Lady to her humanitarian efforts, Michelle can make individuals feel as if they've known her forever. Her approach to building rapport stems from authenticity and genuine interest in connecting with individuals of various backgrounds.

Michelle demonstrated her uncanny rapport-building ability in her "Let's Move!" campaign, designed to combat childhood obesity and promote healthier lifestyles for children. She effortlessly connected with children and families by actively listening, sharing personal stories, and showing empathy - she ensured every person felt heard, understood, valued, and cared about by addressing struggles or aspirations with understanding, compassion, and care. Her dedication to understanding others' experiences helped drive its success.

How to build rapport

Building rapport, as we have seen, plays an integral part in both our professional and personal lives, creating strong relationships and efficient communication. Employers tend to favour candidates who can connect with others and fit in seamlessly within existing teams. Similarly, personal relationships flourish when there is an established sense of closeness and understanding, achieved by building rapport.

As soon as we meet someone new, building rapport begins. Small talk offers us the perfect opportunity to discover commonalities and form bonds that transcend cultural boundaries. We tend to gravitate towards those who resemble us or share similar interests, which is why it becomes easier to form rapport when dealing with people who are like us or share similar interests. This does *not* make it impossible to build a rapport with someone vastly different from us. Meaningful connections are still possible without an obvious shared reference point.

Here are some techniques and strategies for building rapport that you can use, even when you struggle to find common ground;

Know yourself - Self-awareness is key. Take time to explore your communication style and leadership approach to get in tune with who you truly are.

Be approachable: Create an environment where team members feel at ease approaching you for help and advice. Don't be on your phone all the time, leave your office door open or wander round and chat to people as you head for a coffee break.

Start with non-threatening conversation starters - opt for "safe topics" during the initial small talk when you make a new connection—talking about shared experiences like the weather or travel plans. Discussing how you arrived at the current location creates an inviting, relatable, and safe atmosphere to connect without anyone feeling pressured or exposed.

Remember names and use them - Nothing says, "Hey, I'm paying attention!" like calling someone by their proper name.

Use humour - When you laugh together, it creates harmony. You can joke about yourself or the situation you find yourself in, but don't make jokes about other people; you will lose credibility and appear mean-spirited, which will create immediate distrust in the other person.

Show genuine interest - Put those active listening skills to good use. Be an attentive listener, pose open-ended questions, and encourage people to open up about their thoughts and dreams - show them that you care about their stories.

That said, it is important that you don't use finding common ground as a cue to immediately take over the conversation by telling long stories about how you are the same or going through the same thing. This will make the other person feel devalued in their own experience. Instead, just find that connection with them inside yourself and let that lead you to a deeper empathy for them, only revealing similarities over time and where appropriate.

Be honest, genuine, and transparent - This cannot be overstated; as the old saying goes, when you tell the truth, you never have to remember what you said to people. Be honest and transparent with your team to build trust. If there is information that you cannot share, come out and say that instead of telling half-truths. You will be respected far more for this approach.

Get personal - Great leaders can make every person in the room feel like they are speaking to them directly, like every person in the room is important. When you know your employees more personally and acknowledge them individually as you speak, they are more likely to support your vision.

Refer to previous conversations - Establish rapport by discussing topics related to what the other person has said previously. Try searching for links between your experiences, interests, or mutual understandings, creating an atmosphere of cooperation and commonality.

Develop ideas together - Show that you value the other person's contributions by expanding upon their ideas, offering insight or suggestions that demonstrate you appreciate their participation and are actively engaged with the conversation.

Come with a non-judgmental attitude - Approach others with an open and accepting mindset. Free yourself of stereotypes and preconceptions to enable genuine understanding and appreciation of their perspectives and experiences.

Disagree respectfully - If you disagree with someone, present your reasons before expressing any disagreement. This will ensure that any differing viewpoint is communicated openly and friendly while still keeping relationships strong and intact.

Recognize and appreciate: Recognize and acknowledge the contributions and achievements of your team members.

Flexibility and adaptability: Be flexible regarding working styles and approaches, accommodating individual preferences wherever possible.

Collaboration and involvement: Engage team members in decision-making and value their input and ideas.

Conflict resolution: Provide positive solutions to disputes by managing them amicably and respectfully. More on this later!

Now we can start putting all these skills to work and test them out "in the field." We'll also be adding on a few more skills that ensure we leave no room for self-doubt. Next up: managing people and teams...

Chapter 10 - Build Like a Leader

"I judge people by what they might be, —
not are, nor will be."

- Robert Browning,
A Soul's Tragedy,
Act II

Once you have mastered your Vision and you have a handle on Strategy, things become clearer, and the ship is much easier to keep on course. Now you can turn your attention to the day-to-day management of the people in your teams.

As a leader, you will most likely never be handed entirely perfect team members who have honed every skill possible and who function as well-oiled machines, as individuals, or as a unit. Quite the contrary. While your team may know what they are doing and have the necessary experience, they will be, like you, on an ongoing journey, learning and growing.

Navigating the skills of **motivation**, **feedback**, and **delegation** are so vital when it comes to working with the 'humanness' of your teams. In this chapter, we are going to jump into developing these skills, focusing on people management.

When I started on my leadership journey, I got this so wrong. Somehow, after being educated in the theory of my chosen profession but never in the human side of managing people, I assumed that when we enter the office environment, we all turn into some kind of robot-like versions of ourselves, leaving all our feelings, characteristics, and personality traits at the door. I, myself, tried to be that way, solely focussed on delivering outcomes on time and within budget, and I expected it from my colleagues. It was all about delivering quality work as efficiently as possible.

Thankfully, as I grew, I realised that this was not only unrealistic, but undesirable too. Albert Einstein couldn't have said it better, "The more I learn, the more I realize how much I don't know." I realised early on that I had a lot to learn when it came to managing people.

One of the main aspects of being a leader is helping your team members to grow as people and motivating them to keep going, building, and improving as they go. You might ask if being a cheerleader is enough. The simple answer is no. There are different techniques, which we will explore, that are designed to help you keep your team members striving for excellence; however, for improvements to be continuous and motivation to be sustained, we must learn as we go along. How do we learn to improve? Though feedback, for one.

For example, there are no motivational rewards that you will get when you touch a hot stove plate, but I assure you that the feedback you receive (a burn blister on your finger) will teach you not to touch a hot stove again. It does not end there; that same learning is also transferred and will help you to recognize and handle similar situations in the future, you will probably be careful about touching anything that appears to be hot in the future, so a single point of feedback will have ripple effects through different areas of your life. The simple nature of learning through giving and receiving feedback correlates directly with your world as a leader. Yes, the cheerleader is important to keep morale up, but, when you couple that with feedback, you will effectively encourage your team members and contribute to their development and success.

Lastly, we will look at delegation. Now, without delegation, there would be no need for motivation or feedback, as you would not be relying on anyone else to assist you. Delegating tasks is fundamentally the first step that you can take as a leader to develop your team members, allowing them the opportunity to learn and build themselves.

Encouraging and motivating others

Have you ever wondered what is the best way to motivate others? Is it by giving free lunches, paying them more, offering stock options, or perhaps threatening them with 'worst case' outcomes if they don't perform well enough?

All of the above, which we will see throughout the rest of this book, is not how modern-day leadership works. Today, in a shifting world where many employees are re-evaluating how they want to live and how they expect to be treated, even (maybe especially) in the workplace, there is a new trend in leadership and motivation that is proving to be much more effective, and it does not cost a thing.

The secret? It is as simple as having a positive attitude and seeing the glass as half full. Instead of always focusing on what can go wrong, what did go wrong, and all the problems you must solve, a 'positive attitude' leader focuses on the vision, is determined to remain positive, to turn every challenge into an opportunity, and to rally the entire organization to work with enthusiasm, having a good time and sparking the genius in everyone around her. Don't get me wrong; I am not talking about 'toxic optimism,' where you refuse to look at problems; I am talking about maintaining a positive attitude while being reasonable and logical throughout challenges.

We all know that leader who instinctively knows how to give people hope; she has a deep-seated belief that there are no problems, only opportunities, and she knows that there is always a way to get things done and that the next great thing is just around the corner. This leader focuses on her team members' strengths, harnessing positive, creative, and productive energy from everyone to catapult the business to success.

Here's the thing, all organizations have this in common – if leaders start looking for problems, they will find them, and very quickly at that. Everyone will be drowning in negativity, and it is easy to go into a downward spiral of fear, worry, and doubt. If the leader does not lead with positivity, it wouldn't be long before the entire workplace turned into a boiling pot of negativity and anxiety.

If, however, you can see the goodness in the business and the people, and you can put energy into increasing the goodness, the team will follow your lead, become more engaged, and they will naturally put more of themselves into their projects, raising the entire organization to a new level of productivity and competitiveness.

This sounds like a dream, right? A positive environment where you can have open conversations, where creativity flourishes, and where problems are transformed into solutions. It is a place where people are so aligned that they reach agreements easily, feel heard, and have the sense that they are so creating. Imagine being the leader who creates a positive and appreciative environment like this.

Imagine being Susan...

Susan is the CEO of a fast-growing tech startup. If you have ever worked in a tech startup, you may know they often suffer from cutthroat leaders with few people- or leadership skills; usually, these are technical founders insisting on serving as CEO so that they will retain their power despite lacking many people or leadership capabilities themselves. Susan, however, stands out as an exceptional example of positive leadership because she recognizes that motivation and optimism are her secret weapons to leadership.

Let's look at how she does things, firstly she is friendly and enthusiastic whenever she communicates with her team and when she gets the chance (which is regularly), she shows genuine interest in their lives, asking about the things she knows are important to them and remembering key things about their lives as they open up to her.

She has her finger on the pulse of every person's workload, making sure to check in on team members whom she knows are under a lot of pressure, and checking in regularly for early signs of burnout and nipping such problems in the bud when they rear their heads.

Susan also manages herself exceptionally well, she knows that she cannot pour from an empty cup and to lead well, she first must make sure she manages herself. She has a solid self-care routine and whenever she feels even a little bit overwhelmed, she takes a break, goes for a short walk, or listens to relaxing music for a few minutes. She meets with a leadership coach every month and makes sure she has enough downtime, this helps her to stay mentally, and emotionally healthy.

One of her greatest strengths as a positive leader is that she gives her teams ample opportunities for development and growth, rewarding them with new challenges and responsibilities when they excel and sending them on special business trips, like conferences, where they represent the company to help them learn and grow professionally.

She mentors and coaches her team like a seasoned professional, scheduling regular one-on-one feedback meetings where she gives guidance, and support. The team thrives in the atmosphere of individual attention and each person sees personal and professional growth as they evolve in the friendly and supportive work environment.

Susan is more than a cheerleader and motivator; she's also an inspired visionary leader and she knows exactly how to paint a vivid picture of the company's future, communicating it clearly in a way that inspires action in her teams.

Techniques and quick tips for encouraging and motivating others

As you read through the techniques below take a moment to mentally note how you can use them to build on your own skills and develop your leadership style:

Become more optimistic: A positive approach toward any situation helps to boost business and engage people to work enthusiastically. Find ways to build your team members' resilience and optimism during challenging times. Lead by example, and like Susan; you will find that people tend to embrace positive leadership much more readily than negative leadership.

Appreciate your employees: To build an effective and successful business, you must build a network of trusting and confident employees. The core of a good relationship between yourself, the leader, and your team members is based on admiration and mutual respect. Appreciating someone means recognizing and valuing their positive qualities, actions, and contributions. Reminding them that their work is meaningful.

How do you show appreciation? A simple acknowledgment when someone has gone the extra mile is all it takes. Even when the overall outcome of a project is not successful, you can show your appreciation for the effort and energy your team has put into it.

Small gestures of gratitude: Gratitude goes beyond just acknowledging efforts; it is about feeling thankful and expressing a sense of deep appreciation. Gratitude is the best way to show people how their presence and work have made a positive impact, and a great leader builds a strong relationship with team members by showing gratitude and genuinely praising what they do for the company's success. Hand-written thankyou notes go a long way and publicly thanking someone for their contributions will make them feel appreciated, and more motivated than anything else.

Reward greatness with opportunity: One of the greatest gifts you can give to a team member who constantly excels in their job is to provide them with an opportunity for growth. This will help get them closer to their goals and make them feel more hopeful about their future.

Evaluate performance: Evaluating your employees' work helps them to improve their shortcomings. It presents an opportunity to interact with team members one-on-one and help them develop in the specific areas they are struggling with. Your employees will feel more loyalty toward you as a leader.

Create a friendly environment: People feel comfortable and self-motivated where they can freely communicate their short and long-term goals. How can you create such an environment? It is quite simple, really: Openly appreciate your team's work, make time for personal one-on-one interactions, create opportunities, respect your employees, build a trustful and friendly bond with them, and allow them to speak freely without being shut down or criticized, same as you would do outside of work. It is that simple.

Encourage autonomy - Autonomy is one of the greatest desires of most employees, nobody likes being micromanaged, and when you create a framework within which people can work autonomously, your team thrives. We will look at this in more detail in the next two chapters.

Set clear goals - When people have clear goals, they are more motivated, and when they reach their goals, it gives them a sense of accomplishment, builds their self-esteem, and makes them want to do even better.

Encourage work-life balance - This can help prevent burnout, the number one motivation killer.

Lead by example - Employees will watch your every movement closely, and they will do what you do, not what you say. So, if for example, you tell them to be optimistic, but you are always complaining about what goes wrong, your words will have no impact.

Encourage team collaboration - As they say, 'teamwork makes the dream work.' Once a team works together in a practical and comfortable rhythm, they become capable of much more than the total of their abilities, and, as a bonus, they enjoy work more because of the shared experiences they have with colleagues.

Giving and receiving feedback

You might cringe at the thought of having to give, or receive feedback, due to its negative connotation and the stigma linked to it. However, as we go through the types of feedback, you'll realize that it is most likely the delivery of the feedback that you fear most. This fear, if not addressed, can deprive you of essential listening opportunities, but thankfully, you can quite easily overcome this resistance when you learn how and when to deliver constructive feedback.

Whether you love or hate it, providing and receiving feedback is essential for helping employees learn, develop, and ultimately meet their personal and company objectives. When you give feedback the right way, it will help people to work more effectively and be more inspired.

The feedback process must be circular, by that I mean that both you and your team must have the freedom to give and take not only positive but constructive feedback as well. As a leader, you must normalize feedback and treat your teams in such a way that they begin to trust that it is not a way to diminish their value. Over time they will see that feedback is a way to give them opportunities to get better, and so the feedback culture will begin to grow, and you will start noticing a more collaborative and open work culture developing.

Feedback is often avoided simply because it causes inner conflict. You see, we all have these two fundamental human needs: the drive to learn and develop (by taking feedback onboard and improving) and the desire to be accepted for who we are (wanting to be right and perfect all the time and not to receive criticism). This reality makes feedback a tricky matter and getting it just right is a constant balancing act.

In the book, *The Art of Possibility: Transforming Professional and Personal Life,* the famous musical conductor Benjamin

Zander tells the story of how he first started encouraging feedback from orchestra members. Now, to understand the significance of what he did, you first have to know that the role of the orchestra conductor is, as Zander explains, "one of the last completely authoritarian roles still out there." When leading an orchestra of a hundred or more musicians, the conductor's word is the law; he determines how a musical piece is interpreted, the tempo, and how each musician will contribute, and conductors are known to not take kindly to any type of feedback unless it is positive.

One day, Zander noticed a violin player who he knew quite well looking distracted and uninterested in the music they were playing. Not used to her withdrawn demeanour, he approached her and asked what was amiss. She shared with him that she was struggling to keep up with the fast tempo of a piece at certain parts; she felt overwhelmed and couldn't perform at her best. She also thought that the tempo wasn't doing justice to some of the best parts of the music. Zander took her feedback, and during their next rehearsal, he slowed down the tempo in the parts she pointed out. She was surprised at the unusualness of a famous conductor taking feedback from a single musician. This gesture made her come alive during the piece, and she performed brilliantly. She thanked him afterward for taking her feedback and incorporating it into the piece. On his next visit to this specific orchestra, where he was a regular guest conductor, he found the entire orchestra playing together more harmoniously and following his conducting even more flawlessly than before. The news of his exceptional leadership spread throughout the orchestra and built a new level of trust and connection with the entire team.

In time, and because of this incident, Zander developed a habit of leaving a blank paper on the stand of every musician of every orchestra he conducted, allowing each musician the opportunity to provide feedback on his conduction. He read every piece of feedback, realizing that many of these musicians were world-class artists in their own right and often had very close connections and extensive training in the pieces they were playing. He came to value their input and started implementing the feedback during rehearsals and concerts, often making eye contact with the artist who gave the feedback. He revelled in the excitement and pride he saw in the faces of the musicians as they discovered that their suggestions were being used. Their creativity was appreciated, and their genius came to life with every such implementation. This simple practice has endeared him to the musicians he works with and has elevated his career to inspire greatness in individual musicians because they feel heard.

Feedback Types

Here are some types of feedback to help us better understand how to give and receive it:

1. **Positive feedback:** Positive feedback is when you praise someone for a job well done, and when you notice improvements in their work, and let them know what they did well. Positive feedback is quite easy to give when you look for the good in others, and it is essential because your team must see that you balance both positive and negative.

   A word of caution, when giving positive feedback, make sure that you are authentic in your feedback; the old school 'feedback sandwich' does not work unless you are genuine in your positive feedback, and underestimating your team members' intelligence by placing negative feedback between two fake compliments will do more harm than good.

2. **Constructive feedback:** This is when you notice something is amiss in a team member's performance

or work ethic for example, and you address it directly with the person to give them the opportunity to improve.

3. **Formal feedback:** Formal feedback is often recorded and given in a planned meeting where both parties are fully prepared for questions and react wisely to the discussion topic. A formal performance assessment is an example of this. Formal feedback may include both positive and constructive feedback.

4. **Informal feedback:** Informal feedback is continuous, in-the-moment mentoring provided to team members to equip them with a clear picture of how they did throughout the year. Again, informal feedback may and should include both positive and constructive feedback.

Use the right type of feedback: Your feedback must be accurate to be effective, and this means that before you speak, you must analyse the situation and carefully decide whether to go with positive or constructive feedback. If you find, for example that the timing is not right for constructive feedback, but you have already initiated a conversation, rather use the time to provide positive feedback (if you have authentic positive feedback to give). Using the wrong feedback method in a situation may demotivate people by instilling a negative connotation to feedback. It may leave someone thinking their work is never up to your expectations.

Feedback Timing

Think of a time when you created a presentation of a document. You may have spent hours on the concept and done loads of research; finally, you get the framework right, draft the outline, and place the information logically that conveys the story you want to tell. This is the right direction you are taking. You decide to show it to your manager, proud of the breakthrough you have made, before you dive into finer details - like spell checks, grammar, and formatting. Instead of looking at how far you have come, creating a framework and outline from a sea of unorganized information, your manager starts criticizing the document's layout and pointing out grammatical errors. How will this feedback make you feel? Will you feel like continuing with the project, or will you feel deflated and unmotivated?

Feedback is only effective if given at the right time when the team member, or the leader is in a place where they can accept it constructively.
Here are some things that you should consider when choosing a time for feedback:

- Are both parties ready for the feedback? You can check if someone is ready for constructive feedback by noticing how open they appear. Is their body language receptive or closed off? Do they seem willing to listen, or are they avoiding you or chattering? Are they in a stable emotional state?
- Are both parties in an active mind state, fully engaged, attentive, and mentally present in the moment? Are both actively participating and focused on the conversation at hand?
- Is either party in a heated emotional state? I love this quote which is applicable here... "You cannot see your reflection in boiling water. Similarly, you cannot see the truth in a state of anger. When the water is calm, clarity comes." - Madhu Verma.

Having a polite tone during feedback: Saying the correct thing harshly will not convey your message any better. Instead, use a courteous and respectful manner when giving feedback to team members; this will help them absorb it and feel keen to improve their flaws. By contrast, harsh and mean delivery of feedback will make team members distance themselves from you, creating a gap of distrust and making true cooperation impossible.

Always be direct during feedback: When both parties are ready for feedback, be straightforward about what you want to say. Being direct does not mean you have to be rude; it just means you must be honest, which can be done in a kind and respectful way. Be careful, however, of being overly friendly to make up for harsh feedback; say what needs to be said, using the appropriate facial expressions (for example, do not smile when a stern look is needed); otherwise, you may undo the hard work of having the conversation by being overly apologetic or nice afterward, leaving the team member confused about what you meant.

Vagueness also only leads to confusion, so take the time to craft your message so that there is no doubt about what you are saying.

Be objective - It is best if you can peg your feedback against measurable criteria. Describe the situation you observed, the person's specific behaviour, and then the impact that it had; this will help ensure that you don't get personal and that you remain objective.

Use open-ended questions - After giving feedback, encourage the person to assess themselves and reflect on the feedback by asking questions like: "How do *you* think the project went?".

Offer solutions and support - Don't leave the team member feeling helpless, instead empower them with a solution, like training, reading recommendations, or mentorship, to help them live up to their potential.

Keep it private and don't share feedback amongst team members - Even if you think it won't do any harm and that the person you are sharing information with won't say anything, the person who received the feedback will be on the lookout for signs that you shared this with others, especially if they are embarrassed by the feedback. The slightest hint that you broke their confidence will not go unnoticed and will hurt the relationship between you.

Follow up - After your feedback session, check in on how the other person is doing, this will show your genuine commitment to their development.

Request feedback - Ask for feedback in return and show that you are willing to improve; as we saw in the example above, that kind of leadership is compelling.

On that note, here is my personal feedback request.

If you have constructive feedback to offer me, you can drop me a direct message on my Facebook page;
https://www.facebook.com/newleadershipskills

I welcome all feedback from my readers, and I personally read every message. I am keen to make improvements and ensure this book is a learning aid to as many people as possible.

If, however, you have positive feedback. I.e., this book has given you value and the tools you need to get started, why not share it? pass on your knowledge and show your colleagues, friends and family where they can find the same help?

Simply by recommending the book, sharing the Amazon link, leaving an honest review, or even gifting a copy of the book to your colleagues and team members, you will show others where they too can find the guidance they may be looking for.

QR Codes make it so easy these days to be taken directly where you want to go online, so just point your phone camera at either the UK or the USA QR Code whichever is appropriate for you and it will take you direct to the book's Amazon review page to leave your review (and upload your photo!).

Now where were we? Oh yes… delegation.

The art of delegation

Next, let's look at delegation. What exactly is delegation? Formally it is described as: "Transferring accountability for particular tasks from one person to another." Sounds easy enough, right?

Those of you who have tried delegating without guidance or experience will know that delegation is indeed an art, and it is more complex than passing off tasks to others and expecting to get perfect work back. There are many complexities in the delegation process, from managing the team morale, the abilities of the person you are delegating to, their state of mind, your expectations, doubts and fears, and a myriad of things in between.

As a leader, you may feel that you want to maintain control by doing things yourself, not only to make sure that it is done but also to make sure that it is done correctly. This can be extremely hard to overcome, but to be a great leader, it is inevitable. Doing everything yourself is not the role of a leader, nor will it ever turn you into a master in the art of delegation. As a leader, you need to learn to trust and have faith that you have led and mentored your team members effectively to do the tasks they were hired for and to feel comfortable enough to seek guidance and feedback where necessary.

Delegation is a pivotal aspect of leadership; you need to use it to efficiently allocate and organize resources to achieve greater results than you can ever achieve on your own. As business becomes more complicated and ruthless, the responsibilities placed on leaders and managers grow and change every day. If you do not learn to delegate efficiently, you will most likely find yourself constantly on the brink of burnout, trying to do everything yourself, being frustrated by your lack of success, and feeling growing resentment towards your team members.

In this section, we will discuss some of my favourite tried and tested techniques to develop your delegation skills. But, before we go into the 'how to' of delegation, let's have a quick look at the two different types of delegation:

Delegation for Development	Delegation for Results
Assigning a task to an employee who doesn't have any expertise in it. While there may be someone else in the company who is more equipped for the project, you break it down into small steps and delegate it to new	Prioritizes achieving specific outcomes and meeting objectives within a defined timeframe. In this kind of delegation, the delegate is usually very skilled at the tasks given, the environment is normally the high-pressure kind, and

team members so that they can stretch their abilities. This kind of delegation indicates a long-term commitment toward employee development as you will have to invest time and effort to train them.	the team member must be able to work autonomously (i.e., without any handholding).

Techniques for effective delegation

Employee training: While delegating, you must ensure that your employees or colleagues have the knowledge and skills required to do the work. Skills assessment, followed by training, where needed, before delegation, makes it easier for team members to execute tasks effectively and on time.

Trust in employees: One of the greatest barriers to effective delegation is a leader who has no trust that team members can do the job or task effectively. Developing trust in employees' skills can be built by assessing and training them before the task.

Match tasks to skills and interests - The greatest leaders know what to delegate to whom, and they try to find out what people are passionate about and what they are good at so that they can use people in their "genius zone", where they can do their best work, while also feeling fulfilled.

Delegation needs communication skills: Communication has been covered previously and is vital when delegating. Difficulties usually arise when your employee does not understand the tasks or projects you delegate in the same way you do. This is why you must be very thorough and explain tasks and expectations clearly. Don't assume people will just 'get you'; take the extra time to brief properly, and you will undoubtedly reap the rewards and end up with a happier, more productive team as well.

Clearly define tasks and responsibilities - I suggest creating a written brief for projects. It will take some time to put together, but it will save you time and trouble in the future, empower your teams to work independently and give them the best chance at success.

Managing time: Create and stick to checkpoints and deadlines for team members. Check employee accountability by regularly scheduling time to review compliance with the plan.

After delegation, you need to give feedback: Delegation is not simply transferring the task to the person. As a leader, you must give feedback to the team member to guide them on where they are doing well or where they can improve. To establish effective feedback, you need to monitor, evaluate performance, coach, and give a combination of positive and constructive feedback throughout.

Encourage accountability - When you have set a standard, check that this standard is being met, and immediately call people on any breaches or deviations. This is how you build mutual trust and cooperation in teams.

Delegation in real life - a case study

Let's look at an example of how important delegation is. Cindy is a leader who struggles to delegate. Previously, she didn't know that she had a problem delegating to other people; she assumed that she was doing an okay job, and her failure only became apparent when she was called in for constructive feedback by her manager for not completing work efficiently.

What brought Cindy to this point was a combination of things; she was always worried that her team members were ineffective at completing tasks. She failed to communicate clearly what they should do, and she would just hand off projects to them or give them simple tasks in the hope that they would be able to do them properly, but knowing in the back of her mind that it was going to be incomplete in the end.

As deadlines approached, she would find herself panicked and fluttering around her team, causing them to become nervous and even more ineffective. Her team members were constantly on edge and became demotivated, which resulted in them often not completing the tasks she did give them.

While this happened and the work became a crisis, Cindy would try to help and complete the tasks herself. She ended up overextending herself and, most importantly, becoming distracted from what she should be doing, which is leading. This nearly led to her losing her job.

Thankfully, once Cindy realized, through constructive feedback what her problem was, she learned to improve her delegation techniques. Her company sent her on a leadership training course, realizing that they had thrown her into the deep end of management too soon and that she still had lots to learn. She quickly learned to trust her team and give clear communication and expectations of what she wanted from her team members and over the next few months, her career took a turn for the better, as she became a more effective delegator.

Cindy implemented an open-door policy, started incorporating regular feedback, and allowed team members to come and talk to her if they were having problems. She implemented regular check-ins, building accountability in her delegation and keeping a pulse on what was going on.

* * *

When multiple people become a team, and responsibility falls on the teams' shoulders, delegation can be your best friend. So, it's worth taking the time to get it right.

Next, we will look at what happens when delegation is done badly, and you find yourself compelled to micromanage!

Chapter 11 Micromanaging. We Don't Do That Here

"The best executive is the one who has sense enough to pick good men to do what they want done, and self-restraint enough to keep from meddling with them while they do it."

- Theodore Roosevelt

The Urge to Micromanage

Micromanagement is a term that is used not only often but loosely as well. We ask: where is the line really? When are you *micromanaging,* and when are you just *managing well*? What is the right amount of management?

This is the best definition of 'micromanagement' that I have found: *"where a supervisor closely tracks or directs the work of employees or subordinates."* That may sound quite harmless, but we also know that micromanagement is known for, and is driven by, the urge to control. So then, a micromanager is a manager who acts from the need to control the other person.

We look at the effects of this style of management. What does this type of controlling behaviour do to people? What is the real price of micromanagement? Is it ever effective?

Simply put, micromanagement destroys the backbone of any organization. It is hugely destructive and without a doubt one of the worst problems a team can face. The micromanager always tries to over-control the team members to get tasks done, instead of learning the skills that we discussed in the last chapter - delegation. Most people, when confronted by a micromanager, will find it hard to pinpoint exactly what makes them unhappy about their work circumstances. Generally, these employees tend to feel that the company is attempting to eat up more of their resources than they are entitled to.

What causes a leader to micromanage? Micromanagement is often a sign of an inexperienced manager who attempts to make up for a lack of experience with controlling behaviour. While the micromanager may find satisfaction in the sense of control they gain, the employee's creativity will be suppressed, time will be wasted on monitoring unimportant minutiae, and an unpleasant work atmosphere will be the result.

You may well know micromanagers yourself or have struggled with micromanaging behaviour. Around 59% of workers have, at one point in their careers, worked under a micromanager. 79% of these people said that micromanagement hindered their ability to accomplish their duties, and 85% claimed that it had a bad influence on their morale. About 36% of employees admitted that they switched jobs due to micromanagement.

What are the effects of Micromanagement?

In the short term, micromanagement might achieve results, but in the long term, it has destructive outcomes that could be fatal for an organization. The employee working under the supervision of a micromanager loses their autonomy, which presents a major problem since, as we have seen throughout this book, one of the main factors influencing employee engagement is the ability to work autonomously.

Overall, micromanagement is like a cancer to the health of any organization. It erodes and undermines the value of every employee and team dynamic. It must, at all costs, be addressed quickly, efficiently, and with deep understanding.

Left unchecked, you should expect the following;

Decreased productivity: The dictating behaviour of the manager not only wastes precious time but will also lower the productivity of employees. We all know that feeling of having someone looking over your shoulder, the way it makes you feel nervous and causes you to work slower and make mistakes. No one likes feeling like that, especially not the person who is being micromanaged.

Lowered morale: When teams are micromanaged, the people in the teams are generally not content, and the morale of the entire team will suffer. The atmosphere in the workplace will be stifled and strained.

Decreased teamwork: When there is a micromanager in the lead, employees do not experience working as a team since every team member already uses their energy to work individually with the leader. Micromanagement forces teams to work separately instead of cohesively together as a unit.

Lack of employee retention: Working under a micromanager makes employees frustrated and unhappy. As time passes, you will see employees leave the company, usually when they can no longer tolerate the controlling behaviour of the leader. I once worked with a brilliant intellectual who many people wanted to work for, because of his grand vision, but he failed to articulate the vision well and instead opted for micromanagement. Most employees would join the team with excitement only to be driven away within 12-24 months because they could not stand being controlled any longer. He would often try to coax the team members to stay by offering them more money, but time and again, that failed. This is because, in the long run, people value autonomy and being treated well much more than monetary rewards.

Limited growth of employees: The major concern of micromanagement is that it suppresses the growth and creativity of employees. The dictatorship of a leader demotivates people and breaks trust, employees start to feel unskilled and incompetent, and they may even give up trying completely.

What causes leaders to become micromanagers?

Now that you have seen the devastating effects of micromanagement, you may be wondering to yourself why, as a leader, anyone would opt for this management style? As with most human behaviour, the answers can be somewhat complicated, and the causes can range across a spectrum of issues. Here are some of the reasons why managers turn into micromanagers:

Fear of losing control: Leaders might micromanage due to a fear of losing control. This is something that is quite prevalent now since working dynamics have moved to a mostly digital setup. Managers often no longer share physical space with team members, and it can quite easily create the feeling of "losing a grip on the team". The natural response to this, for many people, is to tighten that grip and start micromanaging.

Dominion over information: When you have all the information relating to a project or a subject, as the leader, you may feel like you are the only one who can handle the information and that no one else can interpret or organize it correctly. This can cause you to become controlling over the information and, as a natural result, the project, and your team members.

Avoiding feedback: Micromanagement can be used to avoid feedback. When a leader, instead of taking feedback and changing what needs to be changed, ignores the feedback from the employees, they choose not to communicate with them properly and turn to controlling behaviour instead.

5 ways leaders can break the habit of micromanagement

Do you recognise yourself in any of the descriptions of micromanagers? If you do, firstly don't get too upset with yourself; we have all been there at some point. The first step, as with most bad habits, is to realize and acknowledge that you have a problem. Now that you have that awareness, let's look at some of the ways that you can start breaking that habit and start building a stronger team and business going forward:

Don't get overwhelmed by low-priority activities: Micromanagers invest their time in low-priority activities, which means they are easily overwhelmed. Good managers should focus on the bigger picture, those big deals, and the future strategy of the company The only way to do this is by delegating minor details to the team. Take those first steps and start delegating tasks to employees. Not only will this free up your time to do the big picture stuff, but it will also boost the self-confidence and morale of your team and make them feel even more motivated.

Stop obsessing over every choice and change: Knowing the entire business and figuring out every solution yourself is not your purpose as a leader, nor is it your responsibility. Remember: you have teams for a reason, and once you allow them freedom, autonomy, and permission to bring their own genius into projects, you can enjoy the benefits of becoming a stronger leader. Stop obsessing, allow others to help you, and things will start changing.

Practice being happy with the work of your teams: If you are a micromanager, you probably find that you are never satisfied with the work of your team. You may even catch yourself thinking, often, that no one can do the work better than you can. Fortunately, this is rarely ever completely true. This brings us back to delegation: When you delegate work with proper guidelines, your employees will often flourish. If you can start to better appreciate their efforts, and help them improve where they need to, then you will be able to enjoy the journey and fruits of the labour without the overwhelm of having to micromanage every small detail.

Make inclusion the cornerstone of every conversation and decision: As a leader you can suppress the need or desire to micromanage by communicating with your team members and by inviting them to share their feedback freely. You should delegate the task at hand to a suitable subordinate and help them to make decisions under your supervision through guidance, and of course, good, open communication.

Stop confusing accountability with micromanagement: If you are a micromanager, you are probably telling yourself that by micromanaging you are keeping your team accountable.

This is an easy mistake to make and a good attempt at justifying controlling behaviour, especially if you don't know better. Now that you understand micromanagement and its effects better, you can unlearn this behaviour. By delegating properly, as we have explored in the previous chapter, you can become a more effective manager and leader.

Is Micromanagement Ever Appropriate?

As you have probably realized from the information in this chapter, micromanagement is not conducive to a happy career and a thriving business, but there are some situations where it could be justified as a strictly temporary measure, and even then, micromanagement should be implemented very carefully. Let's look at what this looks like and when it can be considered:

- When you are working on an extremely high-stakes project or a critical task where there is zero margin for error.
- When you are dealing with new or inexperienced employees, and they still need close guidance and plenty of training.
- When you are facing a temporary crisis.
- If your industry is highly regulated and strict adherence to procedures is required.

Let's explore an example: say you have a situation where, in the short term, a particular project is not going in the right direction, and micromanagement becomes the only way to get the project over the finish line. You can probably see how this can become a very slippery slope for conflict or repeat behaviour. Firstly, if you have tendencies towards micromanagement, you may think that every project is a crisis, and you will want to use that to justify micromanagement all the time. Keep a check on this and avoid micromanaging, except in the most isolated cases understanding that if micromanagement becomes necessary, true leadership has failed.

If you are in this situation, the way to successfully micromanage a project over the finish line is for the micromanager to come in, analyse what is wrong in the project and suggest methods for it to be fixed. Communication in this process is crucial; this will make the difference between having a disgruntled and disempowered team and having a team that rallies to get the project completed, willingly giving up some autonomy in the short term for the greater good. As the manager, you should carefully involve the people who are at that point responsible for the task so that they maintain a sense of ownership, responsibility, and autonomy over the project.

After the problem is resolved, you then must step back and leave the project to be run by your teams.

What to do instead of micromanaging?

Firstly, remember that the need to stop micromanaging is not about you. It is about your team. It is for the sake of your team and its success as a cohesive unit that all micromanaging behaviour must be nipped in the bud.

For those of us that have been micromanaging for a long time, it can be a difficult process. You may not know any other way to manage, and even if you learn new management techniques and skills, it will take some time and effort to step away from it. Earlier in this chapter, we looked at a few quick methods to break the habit of micromanaging. Now, let's look a bit deeper into what it will take to break free of micromanaging forever, so that you can really step into your full potential as a leader.

Most importantly, you must learn to respond intelligently. This means that you need to stop making decisions for your team, and instead, you need to focus on creating and articulating a vision of where the business is going so that they can make the necessary decisions themselves. This vision will act as a road map and will be the tool you all rely on to build trust and cohesion.

Here's what you need to do to fully address a bad micro-management habit:

Reflect on your behaviour: Explore the reasons *why* you feel the need to micromanage. Do you feel as if your employees cannot complete the task in front of them efficiently? Do you fear the potential of subpar performance or ineffective results? It is important for you to identify exactly what your role is within a project and to articulate, even to yourself, why exactly you are involved. Remember that too much interference limits the growth of the team and seriously restricts your potential as a manager.

Get feedback: Micromanagement can breed from a lack of upward communication. Team members feel intimidated or ignored, which means they cannot effectively offer you feedback. This, in turn, creates an environment in which you feel that the disconnect between your instructions and the end results are too large and you end up stepping in to micromanage. Allow your team to communicate with you, free of the fear of retaliation, and welcome insights and feedback on how your management and instruction is being received.

Prioritize what matters and what doesn't: Focus on the bigger picture. It may be easier said than done, but the truth is that managers need to hold on to the vision - the collective vision of every team member's contribution as parts of the whole. Not only do you need to use this to create appealing objectives for your individual team members, but you need to be able to discern the difference between needing to interfere and needing to inspire. Make sure that you are only ever acting when it is effective to do so and that you stick to offering support when that is more appropriate. Keep everyone on track by reminding the team of the task at hand and what the priority value tasks are throughout.

Talk to your team: Communication - and effective communication at that - is critical for strong management. Without clear lines of communication and transparent interactions, the team becomes confused and may cause you to feel as if they cannot be trusted to fulfil tasks independently. I.e., without your interference. When you talk to your team in a productive way, you can leverage their best without micromanaging.

Step back slowly: It may be difficult at first to control your micromanaging urges, so back off gradually. No bad habit can be overcome instantly; it takes time. A micromanager must step back slowly so as not to create discomfort for themselves or their team. When you have a clear picture of what is important to you and what is good for team growth, you learn how to manage things appropriately.

Build trust: When people think that you don't trust them, they lose their decision-making power, they depend on you to do their thinking for them, and they hesitate before taking on any new project or task. A good leader creates a trust-based relationship with their employees and assures them that they believe in their abilities to work effectively. The simplest way to build trust is to tell your team that you trust them and that you are confident that they can do the work efficiently.

The right fit: A great leader should always know their employee's skills and abilities. Assign each task to the best-matched employee to achieve the greatest outcome. Alternatively, you could choose to involve an employee that is still learning the skill and shows promise in this area but put strict boundaries in place about your involvement to minimise the urge to micromanage.

Know your employee's limitations: Sometimes managers labour on the smallest details and overreact to minor mistakes. Doing so may make it tempting to pull the employee from the task, but it blatantly ignores the opportunity to help the employee grow - which is what great leaders do. Make sure you are aware of your team's abilities beforehand so that you can plan for the need to intervene without micromanaging the process.

Timing matters: Knowing when to step in and when to simply offer advice or instruction is the key difference between an ineffective manager and a great leader. Make sure that you understand your team members' processes and working style to determine the right time and approach to offer your insights and always offer the employee the opportunity to course-correct before stepping in.

Gauge your involvement: The best way to rework micromanagement energy is to do a situational evaluation. Ask yourself whether the situation at hand can be addressed without your involvement. If you absolutely need to step in, assess the employee you need to work with and decide if they need immediate, intensive coaching or gradual, intermittent guidance over time.

Now that we have explored the pitfalls of micromanagement and examined strategies for dealing with the habit, we can move on to the final set of skills that you will need to be an effective leader.

Chapter 12 - Manage Like a Leader

---

*"Life is not a solo act. It's a huge
collaboration, and we all need to
assemble around us the people who care
about us and support us in times of
strife."*

- Tim Gunn,
Tim Gunn's Advice for Making It Work
by Tara Parker-Pope

Balance in all things is an essential part of living - this is especially true for the relationships we cultivate as leaders. Coming together to forge a dynamic and powerful team is truly about elevating the humanness of every individual and using it to the advantage of the entire organization.

The four values we are discussing here are **autonomy, accountability, collaboration,** and **conflict management**. Without these four pillars, leadership fails, and the opportunity for greatness in this field is missed. Using these skills, however, in unison, creates a workplace environment that is effective, a team dynamic that is enjoyable, and a leader that brings others up along with them.

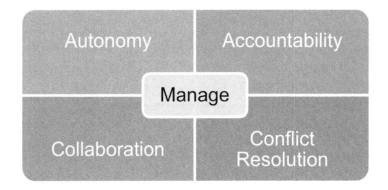

Autonomy

Autonomy seems like a contradiction at first to the ideal of team cohesion. If you aren't involved in the day-to-day workings of your employees, then what exactly are you doing as a leader? Well, the answer is quite simple. Promoting autonomy in the workplace *is* leading - in fact, it is leadership at its finest.

Autonomy in the workplace does not equate to working in isolation or to working without the necessary guidance, collaboration, insight, supervision, and often boundaries that good leadership can provide. Autonomy in the workplace is in fact the foundation of trust, support, and reciprocal behaviour, often resulting in far better performance. It also offers an uptick in happiness and contentment in the lives of your team which in turn creates an environment of productivity.

As we have explored in the previous chapter, nobody likes to be micromanaged at work. Not only does it damage the working relationship, but it removes the employees' ability to self-regulate and bloom into the fullness of their potential. That is why leaders must develop their teams' abilities to function autonomously This is the art of leadership.

Workplace autonomy embraces the concept that every employee is an individual and that this individuality is a strength - a benefit to the organization. We must onboard the belief that every single team member is valid in their approach, insight, and contribution.

In the simplest terms, autonomy in the workplace is offering your employees the freedom to do their jobs. Sounds almost too obvious, right? The thing is, orchestrating the environment that promotes this freedom is often far easier said than done. You need to assess not only the needs and values that align with the organization but measure it against individual team members and their strengths or abilities. You also need to consider the pace of work, the order in which the work is completed, the best motivators for every individual employee, and the strongest management support you can offer - all without slipping into the trap of micromanagement. It's a big ask!

The only real way to succeed in bringing autonomy to the table in the workplace is to invite it - and that requires a strong foundation of leadership trust.

Leadership trust

Building trust as a leader can be incredibly difficult at times and is often a gradual and challenging process. The results however are extremely worthwhile and valuable. Working in a high-trust environment ensures that your employees feel empowered.

By trusting that your employees are highly capable it also empowers you as a leader to be more committed, capable, and compassionate. It is your key to ensuring that your team believes that you are acting in the interest of everyone involved and that you are the right person to steer the ship, so to speak. It demands a give-and-take balance that relies heavily on transparency and communication, which in turn allows your employees to benefit from a shared vision and gives you flexibility when your hands are truly tied in any given situation.

Workplace autonomy versus personal autonomy

Workplace autonomy and personal autonomy are two different creatures. Personal autonomy speaks to the freedom of choice in your personal life that works towards achieving personal goals, the consequences of which are borne by the individual. Workplace autonomy speaks rather to the ability of the employee to make their own decisions within the parameters of working towards a set workplace goal.

This means that workplace autonomy allows the individual the benefit of the doubt, giving them the freedom to drive their own process if it achieves the ultimate end goal. It is an open-ended environment in which the *how* of the matter does not get dictated if the *what* of the matter is achieved. In other words, employees can achieve their goals and complete their work in the way that suits them best as long as the work gets done. The important caveat, of course, is that should the work fail, and the goal be missed, then employees have not only themselves to answer to but the team as well as their leaders (who in turn will have to answer for the results).

The importance of autonomy in the workplace

Now that we know what autonomy in the workplace does, let's explore why it is so important. The first and perhaps the most noticeable effect of workplace autonomy is the atmosphere of trust. Putting faith in your team creates a sense of rightness and allows the organizational hierarchy to function as it should - invisibly. The workplace feels less pressured and chaotic, and employees feel confident and empowered. In fact, the benefits of workplace autonomy are almost countless and have far-reaching positive effects, here are some of the main benefits that can be achieved when we get it right.

Boost productivity

Autonomy means becoming your own motivator. Self-motivated employees are inspired to achieve and are often more likely to engage strongly with their work. The result is a definite increase in productivity where time is spent wisely, and resources are used creatively to ensure results.

Create employee engagement and motivation

Making your own decisions and tackling tasks with an air of trust and freedom is invigorating. It stimulates the mind and gives employees the ability to advocate for themselves. Motivation and engagement naturally follow, and employees that feel trusted by their leaders often deliver above expectations to prove that they deserve the trust they have been granted.

Improve employee retention

Happy employees stay. That has always been and will always be true. Job satisfaction and a positive workplace environment are two of the biggest contributors to employee retention - all of which can be achieved through autonomy in the workplace. High retention rates mean less workplace disruption, reduced use of onboarding resources, and an overall boost to efficiency in the organization.

Develop leadership qualities in your employees

Resilience and self-reliance are two of the most valuable traits a leader can harness. When you promote independent thought and workplace autonomy, these skills are a natural byproduct. These values create the perfect environment for building and uplifting leaders.

Encourage creativity and innovation

Allowing your team the benefit of free thinking means that you are encouraging them to come up with unique and creative solutions. Free thinking breeds innovation, and innovation creates evolution and growth.

How to encourage autonomy at work:

We know what it is and why it is important but how to encourage it? Well, it is better to start slow and small than to expect full autonomy from the get-go.
We've already talked about trust and ditching micromanagement, but there are several other ways in which you can encourage autonomy at work...

Leave room for mistakes: Mistakes happen. Humans are imperfect. Use autonomy in the workplace to stay solution-oriented and turn negative results into a learning experience.

Provide the right tools: Equipping your employees with the tools to be successful ensures that they are starting on the best foot for autonomy and success. It's not just about giving them a comfy chair and twin flat screens. Unhindered access to training, modern software platforms, visibility tools to track their own progress and personnel support systems all form a part of this.

Implement feedback: Ask employees about their satisfaction levels and what can be done to improve them. Implement the feedback you get as much as possible to show your employees that you value their input.

Allow for ownership: Ensuring that employees feel authority and ownership of a project makes them feel motivated to go above and beyond.

An example of good autonomy in action

It is important to remember that people join companies but leave managers. You can be the reason that people stay with your organization. Let's look at an example:

Kevin is an experienced nurse who was just been notified that the hospital he works for is changing his work location. He will be moved from the hospital that is 10 minutes away from his house to a new location that is over 30 minutes from where he lives. Kevin immediately schedules a meeting with his manager where he asks whether it is possible for him to remain at his current location. Unfortunately, even though the manager is empathetic to his situation, he lets Kevin know that the entire team is being moved and that it would be impossible for Kevin to stay at the current location. He reiterates his hope that Kevin chooses to move with the team.

Kevin has a choice to make. He knows that if he says no to moving over, he will lose his job and that if he does say no, he could also look for a different job. If he says yes and goes to the new location, he can either choose to make the best of it, or he could say yes to the new location and be miserable. Kevin knows that he has options and understands that whatever option he chooses, he is personally accountable for the decision.

When Kevin meets with his manager again, his manager reminds him that he is there to support him. Kevin has been growing and thriving as an individual, and his manager has done his best to supply the needed resources. Kevin thanks his manager for the contribution he has made to his personal development. The manager says that he knows it isn't an ideal situation for him and that he has always been a top employee.

He elaborates to explain that while he cannot tell Kevin what to do and it is Kevin's responsibility to decide, he will support him without bias. This is a perfect example of how Kevin remains autonomous and self-directed. Both he and his manager understand that there are choices to be made but that Kevin will be accountable for the choices and that his manager is there to provide him support throughout the transition. In this way, Kevin as an employee remains engaged and relies on his autonomous ability to make the choice.

When employees feel micromanaged or forced into a position, it creates an "I just do what I'm told" mentality, which means that any repercussions or negative consequences are seen as "not their fault". This is not the case for Kevin and his manager because they have a healthy leadership relationship based on autonomy and trust.

Upholding accountability

Accountability is a term that can often cause hesitancy or even fear. The truth of the matter is that for mutual trust and autonomy in the workplace to exist, there still needs to be an understanding of who will be held responsible for any given outcome or held accountable - and specifically for what.
A lack of accountability will negatively affect the team and the organization. One small misstep, unanswered, can quickly snowball into massive problems. Let's look at the following example of accountability:

Melinda has just started as a supervisor at 'Procurements R Us'. She is eager to prove herself and has internalized many of the company's values specifically including safety and quality. Melinda is called into the office because one of the members of the team she manages has made a mistake in an important subcontract document that could delay the project by several weeks. She does not remember seeing the mistake when she checked the document.

Melinda can either blame the employee at fault, perhaps insisting that the mistake was introduced after she checked it

OR she could take on the mantle of responsibility and assure her superior that she will be more diligent in her checks in the future and follow up with the employee.

When Melinda chooses to take accountability, she reinforces the trust that she has earned as well as the commitment to improvement through clear expectations and transparency in communication. She then employs the checks that are required in delegation to ensure continued success in the future.

Delegation, trust, and workplace autonomy are all important and necessary for successful leadership, but so too is accountability. When we as leaders expect and encourage innovation and out-of-the-box thinking, it needs to be met with the understanding that leaders won't hold you accountable for an undesirable outcome but rather for the efforts you made during the project or exercise.

Encouraging Accountability as a Leader

Developing accountability in leadership is not without potential pitfalls. Certainly, there are challenges around embracing empathy and accountability simultaneously for many leaders who seem to believe that showing compassion or sympathy would undermine their ability to hold their team accountable - this is fortunately not true.

Another potential concern is taking on too much responsibility. This is when a culture of accountability goes too far and will result in micromanaging, failed team dynamics, and burnout.

Lastly, there is the issue of setting clear goals for the team. Without knowing who is responsible for what in exact and transparent terms, accountability is impossible. So how does one encourage accountability as a leader?

Invest in leadership development. Make coaching and mentoring an active part of your company culture. Ensure that goals are set clearly and that all lines of communication are kept open. Empower your employees to hold leaders accountable as well - it is a two-way street, and when employees feel confident in their ability to bring feedback to their leaders, it improves the entire team.

Don't play the blame game: Focus on the restorative actions that need to take place rather than who is at fault. Shifting focus in this way ensures that everyone feels able to embrace a culture of accountability.

Remember, the traits of an accountable leader are:

1. Clear and transparent communication
2. Delegation
3. Open listening channels
4. Ownership
5. Investment in your people
6. Quality two-way feedback

Collaboration: Teams That Work Like a Charm

Now that we have looked at autonomy and accountability, we need to look at pulling it all together. That is where collaboration comes in. True collaboration exists when teams use their learned skills and leverage them individually towards group success - in other words, when they come together and problem-solve.

No organization can function properly without the ability to realign and adjust. For this to happen, collaboration and communication need to be core values upheld at every level, from employee to top leadership. So why is it that collaboration plays such an important role? That will be because of the following valuable benefits it provides.

Problem-solving: Teams that collaborate lean on each other for support, and that is especially true when it comes to problem-solving. They leverage the pooled resources, insights, and skills of the entire team to solve problems and are, therefore, more effective, and successful overall... Multiple brains are better than one.

Adaptability: A functioning team, one that strongly relies on collaboration - is also a team that is adaptable and ready to make rapid changes. When teams understand their end goal and function, they can quickly align and adapt to any situation that arises.

Open communication: Constant understanding of where teams are at in terms of progress and responsibilities means that teams move forward as a cohesive unit.

Skill sharing: Collaboration within a team leads to knowledge sharing. Employees learn from each other and teach each other along the way, thus increasing the shared skill base of the whole organization.

Goal alignment: Combining abilities and knowledge to achieve a common goal is the hallmark of collaboration. This encourages team-wide support, increased productivity; and...

Engagement: When you make employee engagement a metric for success, it creates teams that are comfortable sharing ideas and feedback as well as giving individual team members a feeling of satisfaction and willingness to get the work done.

The most important result of collaboration is the effect it has on employees. Collaboration creates happy workers, employees are more efficient, and company morale is boosted. This also encourages cross-team collaboration, a more appealing work environment, and overall improved retention rates. Truly, collaboration is a win-win scenario every time.

How a Leader Strengthens Collaboration

Want to know how to make practical changes that encourage collaboration? Here are three simple ideas to get you started:

Use technology: Think video conferencing, cloud-based sharing, instant messaging, and more - but think of them as the backbone of how your teams operate. Create a system that uses these tools as standard practice, that is introduced at induction. Tools like Asana, Trello and Slack.

Create cross-functional teams: Melding different departments and areas of expertise means thought provocation, creative problem-solving, and holistic decision-making.

Celebrate! Make sure employees know the impact their work has on the organization and acknowledge their individual contributions. Offer praise on successful collaborations and create feedback opportunities for the entire team.

Life-Saving Collaboration

In 2018, disaster struck in northern Thailand when monsoon rains arrived. Twelve members of the Thai Wild Boars soccer team and their coach disappeared amidst the torrential downpours. Members of the community raised the alarm and soon the search grew to over 10,000 volunteers including emergency responders, journalists, and situational experts.

It took every leadership effort not only to perform the diving rescue but to keep the boys alive and calm for the 10 days they were stuck in a cave and cut off from the rest of the world.

Key moments during this event include the decision to notify parents before the media once the team was found as well as the use of the command centre to determine the safest extraction method. The decision was to sedate the team, covering their faces with full oxygen masks, and have a dive team guide them out to avoid an underwater panic.

This event was an amazing example of how different disciplines and levels of authority came together to complete a successful rescue. From the community volunteers all the way up to Governor Osotanakorn. Key leadership, and collaboration skills meant that over ten thousand human beings remained co-ordinated and connected through clear lines of communication.

Resolving Conflicts

The final skill that leaders need to cultivate after ensuring that autonomy, accountability, and collaboration have been addressed is the inevitable need for conflict resolution. In a very dynamic workplace, no matter how cohesive or successful a team is, there will be occasional conflicts. The key is in addressing these conflicts appropriately - both with the right timing and the right approach. If you mess up during conflict resolution, it can lead to bigger problems down the line. However, know that as long as you make an active effort towards addressing festering issues early, it is possible to turn conflict around.

Remember that every individual is exactly that, an individual, and those individual differences naturally create conflict. It is expected and normal. It is your job as a leader to take these conflicts and turn them into opportunities for growth.

When Collaboration Breeds Conflict

The key to increasing the success of collaboration within your team is to ensure that you employ effective conflict management strategies ahead of time. Some examples of conflict within a collaborative team occur when teams are pitted against each other.

Competing motives, mismatched ideals, and power plays for influence are all conflicts that you should expect to manage as a leader, but the "Us Versus Them" mentality is extremely toxic and can result in very negative outcomes.

What is needed is the ability for teams to communicate effectively and offer feedback without the fear of negative repercussions, and/or resorting to character assassination or other negative strategies to get their point across.

Another big factor that will lead to problems from collaboration is ineffective communication - when teams are duplicating or triplicating their work because they do not effectively and clearly communicate their progress with other collaborators.

How to Manage Conflict as a Leader

Managing conflict can require you to use skills that you may not feel comfortable with, at least not yet.

It will require you to learn how to remove yourself from the situation without removing any humanness from the interaction.

There are a few different types of conflict when it comes to the workplace. This also means that there are different ways in which to address them.

The first type of conflict is **task conflict** which often involves issues relating to work assignments, resource division, and sometimes even differences of opinion on policies and procedures. The key here is to manage the expectations of the work and to remove judgments so that you can get a clear interpretation of the facts. Basically, employ the communication, autonomy, and accountability practices we have outlined earlier in the chapter. The best cure here is prevention, but task conflicts can quickly be addressed by returning to these fundamentals.

This type of conflict may be one of the easiest to resolve, the problem however is that it may have deeper roots and more complexity than you first realize. Arguments between co-workers about which one of them should go to a conference for example, or whose responsibility it is to manage a certain task, can be seated in a deeper conflict based on rivalry. Stepping in as a mediator, you as the leader should be able to identify and encourage the deeper interest of the individuals and each party's underlying position. Use active listening - repeating back what you hear, and deeper probing to engage both parties in a collaborative problem-solving process. Solutions developed together, will be more effective.

The second type of conflict that you will deal with is **relationship conflict**. These are mostly based on differences in personality, usually arising between people who do not ordinarily mix in real-life scenarios.

If there is a long-simmering tension between colleagues whether it's over personality differences or other issues you should invite them to get to know each other better. Create opportunities for them to interact socially - this may be more effective than stepping in and trying to resolve the conflict without context.

When they are more comfortable with each other, you can address the fact that they probably have more similarities than they may at first have realized. That sets a better tone that allows you to address the conflict more effectively. Remember not to defend any position but rather demonstrate empathy and interest and invite the parties involved to do the same. Offer them a chance to see it from the other's perspective.

The final type of conflict that you need to be prepared for is **value conflict**, which can be tricky to navigate. It normally arises from a fundamental difference not only in values but in identities. From religion, to politics, to ethics, and other deeply held beliefs, this type of conflict is very sensitive and requires a delicate hand. It often creates a sense of defensiveness before the issue is even raised and can escalate very quickly if left to fester.
Strong values are a sign of a strong person, and that is a good thing to have in your team. However, a value-based dispute has the potential to cause a massive rift which is why you should refrain from choosing sides at all costs.

These disputes are opportunities to highlight universal beliefs and allow each party the freedom to be themselves without feeling the need to adopt the others' beliefs. Remind them that there is often no one right way to feel about these issues and rather encourage them to allow space for the other to exist in harmony. It may be taboo in your organization to discuss these issues; however, you do need to address any conflict that arises from a difference in values.

The Best Strategies to Handle Conflict

Constructive conflict resolution matters because, without it, your team will fail, not only as a cohesive unit but in their ability to succeed within their projects and within the organization. The following strategies will guide you to manage conflict effectively;

- Gather all the information that you can at the beginning of the interaction. You need all the facts at hand before you can open the conversation.

- Explain why it is important to rely on mediation rather than your authority. Everyone must understand that it is best to resolve conflict collaboratively instead of just relying on you to make a snap decision and enforce your decision on them.

- If your colleagues expect you to step in as the boss, make it clear that they are part of a team, and you are there to facilitate growth instead of creating individual actions for which they are personally responsible.

- Ensure that any misunderstandings or poor communication has been resolved and address any biases that may be affecting their interaction.

- Create or choose a neutral space to talk and set ground rules at the beginning. Make sure that each party will be allowed to share their position and then guide them to a resolution.

- Finally, look towards the solution. You may find that working towards a solution together allows the team members in question to dissipate the conflict altogether. When they have common ground and work together to find a solution that is acceptable to both parties, they are more likely to accept the resolution.

There is a grace with which you should balance the four values of autonomy, accountability, collaboration, and conflict because each of these influence each other.
Simply by ensuring that you use these four skills effectively you will achieve a workplace dynamic that makes people *want* to work with you.

Conclusion

As we have seen in this book, title alone does not a leader make. If anything, being a leader is something more than just the sum of its parts - more than managerial tasks, and more than running through the motions of vision-oriented exercises. True leadership is a way of thinking and being that is inspired, innovative, and innately based in truth. You are on the precipice of your greatest leadership transformation - are you ready to put it all to work?

Let's look back at some of the things that we have gleaned from the chapters in this book: One of the first things we learnt, was the nature of leadership, and how it requires a combination of trust, action, perspective, focus, vision, and effective communication skills.
More to the point, we learned that leadership is different from management and that it has nothing to do with your hierarchy or rank.
We learnt that there are two approaches to exerting influence, namely manipulation and inspiration. While manipulation requires incentives and consequences to govern behaviour, inspiration creates a collaborative atmosphere that is based on trust and personal motivation.

Does it feel scary to think of yourself as the voice in charge? We now know that true leadership does not require an extroverted nature; it simply requires a commitment to truth, both in the embodiment of your values through action as well as an inner knowledge of who you are.
Not only is leadership separate from your personality type, but it is separate from gender as well. We've seen that women make excellent leaders with the ability to leverage unique qualities such as communication and conscientiousness.

Challenges that you can expect to face as either a new or experienced leader include the ability to provide inspiration and motivation to others. You need to be able to see your team members as individuals and yet still manage them as a team, manage change, and manage conflict.

Good leadership means making tough decisions, managing a business's resources, delegating responsibilities, and actively seeking feedback. It requires you to overcome internal and self-related challenges such as wanting to be liked, staying positive, remaining calm amidst chaos, learning to trust team members, dealing with anxiety and stress, and even maintaining a human connection. These are all important facets of being a good leader that you are ready to unlock on your own journey.

Leaders will be challenged during any crisis - often faced with the most challenging and demanding situations that you have encountered in your career - you need to learn how to navigate through this uncertainty, sometimes even questioning and challenging your own value system, all to keep your team motivated and focused on achieving the goals at hand. Want to know a secret? You've got this. Remember, we have learned that being a good leader means doing the work to overcome the obstacles of internal and external challenges without losing sight of the humanity of your team or yourself.

Looking back now, you will realize that you've learned a lot more about yourself and have a deeper understanding of what kind of leader you want to be. We explored Imposter Syndrome, how it happens, and why it is that people feel undeserving of their accomplishments and the praise that they receive. There are various aspects at play when it comes to Imposter Syndrome - from external and internal causes as well as several symptoms that you need to look out for. Not only can you now identify Imposter Syndrome, but you can also understand how and why it manifests as well as what to do about it. You can forever say goodbye to that doubtful inner voice - because you know what Imposter Syndrome is and how to kick it to the curb.

Imposter Syndrome, as with most trauma healing, requires dedication, persistence, and focus to wade through an incredibly difficult frame of mind. Let's remind ourselves of some of the strategies for dealing with it:

- Change your mindset and ask for help! - reach out to your mentors, do personal evaluations, and talk to someone who can help you work through your belief patterns.
- Be prepared - exercise caution when showing vulnerability, making sure that there is a distinction between vulnerability and core competency.
- Acknowledge and celebrate your contributions - remember there is an "I" in everything, including team.
- Reach out and ask for affirmation - be honest about where you are in your journey.
- Use the seven-step approach we worked through in Chapter 4 for combating Imposter Syndrome.

Becoming self-made - becoming the CEO of your own life and taking charge - requires you to put the "self" back into your process. Self-care, self-love, and self-awareness are the trinity of building a future you can be proud of. You will also need to embrace self-compassion, self-confidence, and self-leadership as superpowers because they shape how we perceive ourselves and our abilities. Knowing what we are capable of, what we are worth, and knowing your potential to achieve your goals is exactly what you need to be a strong leader and build a successful future. That is the most exciting part of this journey: YOU are at the wheel of your own destiny.

Speaking of the journey, let's look back at the practical side of becoming a great leader: We explored in detail the skills and abilities that you need, that will propel you towards great leadership.

We discussed micromanagement and how not to fall into the traps it presents. Remember: leadership has two distinct facets - thinking and acting. You need to use both in order to lead, to manage, and to connect with your team.

Here are some of the skills that we focussed on for your journey moving forward:

- Self-development skills - empathy and emotional intelligence
- Strategic skills - strategic thinking and communicating a vision
- Planning and action skills - goal setting, problem-solving, and decision-making
- Communication skills - active listening and using effective verbal skills to build a rapport
- People management skills - the cultivation and motivation of others, as well as giving and receiving feedback and delegation
- Team management skills - autonomy and accountability, collaboration, and conflict resolution

With these skills in hand, you are well on your way to great leadership. Give yourself time and grace. Reflect, breathe, and persevere with the progress you are making. Bring out the best leader from within by welcoming feedback, opportunities to learn, and the exciting reality that you can be a great leader in your own right.

More than anything, I want you to accept and welcome yourself as a leader of the future - right now.

Your chance to help others...

Hopefully this book has given you everything you need to get started, I know it's a lot to take in and I debated whether it should have been split into two books instead of one, but here we are, a single comprehensive resource to work through at your own pace.

So, before we conclude, I wish to explain the importance of leaving a review on Amazon. Not only you will show other IS sufferers where they can find the guidance they are looking for, but you will be elevating the visibility of the book to reach people who perhaps have never heard the label before and don't know that help is out there.

Sadly, we now live in a world of AI generated reviews and fake ratings which Amazon works incredibly hard to weed out. One of the ways you can ensure yours is not removed by Amazon is to simply add a photo to your review. A photo of your paperback, your Kindle or if you're feeling brave... you reading it!

So once you have taken the photo, simply point your phone camera at whichever store you bought the book from (UK or the USA) QR codes below – this will take you direct to the review page for this book.

Thank you so much for your support, it is very much appreciated.

Sources and Further Reading

Chapter 1

The Balance SMB. (n.d.). What Is Leadership? Definition and
Meaning. The Balance Small Business.
https://www.thebalancesmb.com/leadership-definition-
2948275
Emergenetics International. (n.d.). 5 Ways to Define
Leadership. Emergenetics. https://emergenetics.com/blog/5-
ways-define-leadership/
Avail Leadership. (n.d.). The Test of True Leadership.
https://availleadership.com/test-of-true-leadership/
IMD. (n.d.). 10 People Mistakes Leaders Make.
https://www.imd.org/research-knowledge/articles/10people-
mistakes-leaders-make/
YouTube. (n.d.). What Makes a Great Leader?
https://www.youtube.com/watch?v=nSUJwmPQEyg
Gleeson, B. (2016, November 9). 10 Unique Perspectives On
What Makes a Great Leader. Forbes.
https://www.forbes.com/sites/brentgleeson/2016/11/09/10-
unique-perspectives-on-what-makes-a-great-
leader/?sh=754bd8e15dd1
Kruse, K. (2013, April 9). What Is Leadership? Forbes.
https://www.forbes.com/sites/kevinkruse/2013/04/09/what-is-
leadership/?sh=4e722dd45b90
Anderson, A. (2015, March 1). The Characteristics of a True
Leader. Forbes.
https://www.forbes.com/sites/amyanderson/2015/03/01/the-
characteristics-of-a-true-leader/?sh=98147e82324d
Fisher College of Business. (n.d.). Why Women Are Better
Leaders. https://fisher.osu.edu/blogs/leadreadtoday/why-
women-are-better-leaders

ConnectAmericas. (n.d.). 6 Features That Define Female Leadership. https://connectamericas.com/content/6-features-define-female-leadership-0

Harvard Business Review. (2018, November). How Women Manage the Gendered Norms of Leadership. https://hbr.org/2018/11/how-women-manage-the-gendered-norms-of-leadership

ProofHub. (n.d.). Women in Leadership Roles: A Comprehensive Guide. https://www.proofhub.com/articles/women-in-leadership-roles

Innosight. (n.d.). 5 Ways to Break Through Innovation Bottlenecks. https://www.innosight.com/insight/5-ways-to-break-through-innovation-bottlenecks/

Chapter 2

Horowitz, B. (2014). The Hard Thing About Hard Things: Building a Business When There Are No Easy Answers (EPub Edition). HarperBusiness. ISBN 978-0-06-227320-8.

BetterUp. (n.d.). Surface-Level Diversity: The Key to Building an Inclusive Workplace. https://www.betterup.com/blog/surface-level-diversity?hsLang=en

Innosight. (n.d.). 5 Ways to Break Through Innovation Bottlenecks. https://www.innosight.com/insight/5-ways-to-break-through-innovation-bottlenecks/

InitiativeOne. (n.d.). Leadership Challenges. https://www.initiativeone.com/post/leadership-challenges

Lifehack. (n.d.). 10 Challenges Leaders Always Face and How to Deal With Them. https://www.lifehack.org/articles/work/10-challenges-leaders-always-face-and-how-deal-with-them.html

Forbes Human Resources Council. (2022, May 23). 14 Challenges and Lessons for New Business Leaders. Forbes. https://www.forbes.com/sites/forbeshumanresourcescouncil/

2022/05/23/14-challenges-and-lessons-for-new-business-leaders/?sh=23565e535b1e

Center for Creative Leadership. (n.d.). First-Time Managers Must Conquer These Challenges. https://www.ccl.org/articles/leading-effectively-articles/first-time-managers-must-conquer-these-challenges/

Chapter 3

Psychology Today. (2017, August). Nine Ways to Fight Impostor Syndrome. https://www.psychologytoday.com/us/blog/how-to-be-yourself/201708/nine-ways-to-fight-impostor-syndrome

Neil Sattin. (2018, March). Change Your Thoughts, Change Your Life: Cognitive Distortions with Dr. David Burns. https://www.neilsattin.com/blog/2018/03/133-change-thoughts-change-life-cognitive-distortions-dr-david-burns/#:~:text=Today%2C%20David%20Burns%20and%20I, you%20can%20%E2%80%9Cfeel%20good%E2%80%9D.

Psycom. (n.d.). Imposter Syndrome. https://www.psycom.net/imposter-syndrome

KPMG. (n.d.). KPMG Study Finds Most Female Executives Experience Imposter Syndrome. https://info.kpmg.us/news-perspectives/people-culture/kpmg-study-finds-most-female-executives-experience-imposter-syndrome.html

Verywell Mind. (n.d.). Imposter Syndrome and Social Anxiety Disorder. https://www.verywellmind.com/imposter-syndrome-And-social-anxiety-disorder-4156469

Glamour Magazine. (n.d.). Ditch the Inner Imposter: Book Extract. https://www.glamourmagazine.co.uk/article/ditch-inner-imposter-book-extract

Impostor Syndrome. (n.d.). 5 Types of Impostors. https://impostorsyndrome.com/articles/5-types-of-impostors/

The Muse. (n.d.). 5 Different Types of Impostor Syndrome and 5 Ways to Battle Each One. https://www.themuse.com/advice/5-different-types-of-imposter-Syndrome-and-5-ways-to-battle-each-one

LinkedIn. (n.d.). Impostor Syndrome: Why Women Leaders Often Fail to Own Their Success. https://www.linkedin.com/pulse/impostor-syndrome-why-women-leaders-often-fail-own-success-buckley/?trk=pulse-article

John Mattone. (n.d.). What Is Imposter Syndrome in Leadership and How Can You Address It? https://johnmattone.com/blog/what-is-imposter-syndrome-in-leadership-and-how-can-you-address-it/

APA. (2013, November). Fraud. https://www.apa.org/gradpsych/2013/11/fraud

BetterUp. (n.d.). What Is Imposter Syndrome and How to Avoid It. https://www.betterup.com/blog/what-is-imposter-syndrome-and-how-to-avoid-it

Parenting For Brain. (n.d.). Overprotective Parents: 5 Common Mistakes to Avoid. https://www.parentingforbrain.com/overprotective-parents/

Skills You Need. (n.d.). Imposter Syndrome: How to Overcome It as a Manager. https://www.skillsyouneed.com/rhubarb/imposter-syndrome-manager.html

Skills You Need. (n.d.). Imposter Syndrome: How to Overcome It as a Manager. https://www.skillsyouneed.com/rhubarb/imposter-syndrome-manager.html

APA. (2013, November). Fraud. https://www.apa.org/gradpsych/2013/11/fraud

KPMG. (n.d.). KPMG Study Finds Most Female Executives Experience Imposter Syndrome. https://info.kpmg.us/news-perspectives/people-culture/kpmg-study-finds-most-female-executives-experience-imposter-syndrome.html

Chapter 4

APA. (2013, November). Fraud. https://www.apa.org/gradpsych/2013/11/fraud

Doist. (n.d.). Impostor Syndrome and the New Manager. https://blog.doist.com/imposter-syndrome-new-managers/

Science of People. (n.d.). Impostor Syndrome: The Complete Guide. https://www.scienceofpeople.com/impostor-syndrome/

CCBHC. (n.d.). 13 Ways to Stop Being a People Pleaser. https://ccbhc.org/13-ways-to-stop-being-a-people-pleaser/

BetterUp. (n.d.). What Is Imposter Syndrome and How to Avoid It. https://www.betterup.com/blog/what-is-imposter-syndrome-and-how-to-avoid-it

Positive Intelligence. (n.d.). Meet Your Saboteurs: The 10 Types of Limiting Beliefs. https://www.positiveintelligence.com/saboteurs/

BetterUp. (n.d.). What Is Failure? https://www.betterup.com/blog/what-is-failure

Verywell Mind. (n.d.). Imposter Syndrome and Social Anxiety Disorder. https://www.verywellmind.com/imposter-syndrome-and-social-anxiety-disorder-4156469#toc-coping-with-imposter-syndrome

Risely. (n.d.). Overcoming Imposter Syndrome at a New Job. https://www.risely.me/overcoming-imposter-syndrome-at-a-new-job/

The Muse. (n.d.). 5 Different Types of Imposter Syndrome and 5 Ways to Battle Each One. https://www.themuse.com/advice/5-different-types-of-imposter-syndrome-and-5-ways-to-battle-each-one

BetterUp. (n.d.). Why Imposter Syndrome Can Be a Competitive Advantage. https://www.betterup.com/blog/why-imposter-syndrome-can-be-a-competitive-advantage

Chapter 5

Kehoe, J. (n.d.). Mind Power into the 21st Century.

Positive Psychology. (n.d.). Self-Leadership: A Complete Guide. https://positivepsychology.com/self-leadership/

Gambill, T. (2021, April 8). Why Self-Leadership Is the Most Important Leadership. Forbes. https://www.forbes.com/sites/tonygambill/2021/04/08/why-self-leadership-is-the-most-important-leadership/?sh=35f3db071ca4

Franko, A. (n.d.). The Essential Role of Self-Leadership. https://amyfranko.com/self-leadership-need/

Positive Psychology. (n.d.). Self-Compassion and Self-Love: A Complete Guide. https://positivepsychology.com/self-compassion-self-love/

BetterUp. (n.d.). The Power of Self-Compassion. https://www.betterup.com/blog/self-compassion

BetterUp. (n.d.). How Self-Compassion Strengthens Resilience. https://www.betterup.com/blog/how-self-compassion-strengthens-resilience

Harvard Business Review. (2020, November). Self-Compassion Will Make You a Better Leader. https://hbr.org/2020/11/self-compassion-will-make-you-a-better-leader

Science of People. (n.d.). How to Be More Confident: 13 Simple Tips. https://www.scienceofpeople.com/how-to-be-more-confident-2/

Harvard Business Review. (2021, February). Don't Let Self-Doubt Hold You Back. https://hbr.org/2021/02/dont-let-self-doubt-hold-you-back

Inc. (n.d.). How to Build Your Confidence as a Leader. https://www.inc.com/young-entrepreneur-council/how-to-build-your-confidence-as-a-leader.html

Skills You Need. (n.d.). Leadership Skills: A Complete Guide. https://www.skillsyouneed.com/leadership-skills.html

Harvard Business Review. (2013, May). Few Executives Are Self-Aware. https://hbr.org/2013/05/few-executives-are-self-aware

Franko, A. (n.d.). The Essential Role of Self-Leadership. https://amyfranko.com/self-leadership-need/

Chapter 6

Verywell Mind. (n.d.). What Is Empathy?
https://www.verywellmind.com/what-is-empathy-2795562
Greater Good Science Center. (n.d.). Empathy: Definition.
https://greatergood.berkeley.edu/topic/empathy/definition
Greater Good Science Center. (n.d.). Why Practice
Empathy?
https://greatergood.berkeley.edu/topic/empathy/definition#wh
y-practice-empathy
Entrepreneur. (n.d.). Why Empathy Is Important in Leaders
Right Now. https://www.entrepreneur.com/growing-a-
business/why-empathy-is-important-in-leaders-right-
now/349575
YourDictionary. (n.d.). Examples of Showing Empathy.
https://www.yourdictionary.com/articles/showing-empathy-
examples
Psychmc. (n.d.). Empathy vs. Sympathy.
https://www.psychmc.com/blogs/empathy-vs-sympathy
6Seconds. (2021, January 20). Empathy vs. Sympathy:
What's the Difference?
https://www.6seconds.org/2021/01/20/empathy-vs-sympathy-
what-the-difference/
Prezi. (n.d.). Case Study: Empathy in the Workplace.
https://prezi.com/0fzrj6ophtzv/case-study-empathy-in-the-
workplace/
Hess, W. (2012, August 21). On Empathy and Apathy: Two
Case Studies. https://whitneyhess.com/blog/2012/08/21/on-
empathy-and-apathy-two-case-studies/
Nieuwhof, C. (n.d.). 5 Reasons Leaders Lack the Critical
Learnable Skill of Empathy. https://careynieuwhof.com/5-
reasons-leaders-lack-the-critical-learnable-skill-of-empathy/
Medium. (n.d.). The Power of Workplace Empathy.
https://medium.com/@humancapitalmagazine10/the-power-
of-workplace-empathy-2c055ebe6c1f
Rock Content. (n.d.). Empathetic Leadership: The Ultimate
Guide. https://rockcontent.com/blog/empathetic-leadership/

HelpGuide. (n.d.). Empathy: A Practical Guide.
https://www.helpguide.org/articles/relationships-
communication/empathy.htm
Tyndale. (n.d.). The Power of Humility and Empathy.
https://www.tyndale.com/sites/readthearc/the-power-of-
humility-and-empathy/
Vocation Matters. (2021, February 2). A Call for Empathy
and Honesty. https://vocationmatters.org/2021/02/02/a-call-
for-empathy-and-honesty/
Harvard Business School Online. (n.d.). The Role of
Emotional Intelligence in Leadership.
https://online.hbs.edu/blog/post/emotional-intelligence-in-
leadership
SHRM. (2018, March). Emotional Intelligence Is Key to
Outstanding Leadership. https://www.shrm.org/hr-
today/news/hr-magazine/0318/pages/emotional-intelligence-
is-key-to-outstanding-leadership.aspx
Kellogg Insight. (n.d.). Why Leaders Should Nurture Their
Social-Emotional Intelligence.
https://insight.kellogg.northwestern.edu/article/why-leaders-
should-nurture-their-social-emotional-intelligence
SlideShare. (n.d.). Case Study of Arun's Emotional
Intelligence. https://www.slideshare.net/SophiyaPrabin/case-
study-of-aruns-emotional-intelligence
HelpGuide. (n.d.). Emotional Intelligence (EQ).
https://www.helpguide.org/articles/mental-health/emotional-
intelligence-eq.htm
MindTools. (n.d.). Emotional Intelligence.
https://www.mindtools.com/ab4u682/emotional-intelligence
MindTools. (n.d.). Emotional Intelligence in Leadership.
https://www.mindtools.com/ax3ar6w/emotional-intelligence-
in-leadership

Chapter 7

Positive Psychology. (n.d.). Self-Leadership: A Complete
Guide. https://positivepsychology.com/self-leadership/

Effective Governance. (n.d.). What Is Strategic Thinking? https://www.effectivegovernance.com.au/page/knowledge-centre/news-articles/what-is-strategic-thinking

Harvard Business Publishing. (n.d.). Strategic Thinking: Because Good Ideas Can Come from Anywhere. https://www.harvardbusiness.org/strategic-thinking-because-good-ideas-can-come-from-anywhere/

Chron. (n.d.). Examples of Successful Strategic Thinking. https://smallbusiness.chron.com/examples-successful-strategic-thinking-15924.html

Strategic Thinking Coach. (2014, January 24). Two Case Studies in Strategic Thinking: Rick Pitino and Billy Beane. https://strategicthinkingcoach.com/2014/01/24/two-case-studies-in-strategic-thinking-rick-pitino-and-billy-beane/

Strategic Thinking Coach. (n.d.). Examples of Strategic Thinkers. https://strategicthinkingcoach.com/tag/examples-of-strategic-thinkers/

LinkedIn. (n.d.). Strategy: The Everyday Ingredients of Strategic Thinking. https://www.linkedin.com/pulse/strategy-everyday-ingredients-strategic-thinking-chris-anstead/

CleverControl. (n.d.). Strategic Thinking: How to Develop It. https://clevercontrol.com/strategic-thinking-develop/

Impact Factory. (n.d.). Strategic Thinking for Leadership Success. https://www.impactfactory.com/resources/strategic-thinking-for-leadership-success/

Investopedia. (n.d.). SWOT Analysis: Strengths, Weaknesses, Opportunities, and Threats. https://www.investopedia.com/terms/s/swot.asp

Harvard Business School Online. (n.d.). How to Develop Strategic Thinking Skills. https://online.hbs.edu/blog/post/how-to-develop-strategic-thinking-skills

Management Study Guide. (n.d.). Leadership Vision: Definition and Characteristics. https://managementstudyguide.com/leadership-vision.htm

LinkedIn. (n.d.). The Importance of a Shared Vision.
https://www.linkedin.com/pulse/importance-shared-vision-patrick-r-palmer/
Forbes. (2015, November 20). Marissa Mayer: A Case Study in Poor Leadership.
https://www.forbes.com/sites/mikemyatt/2015/11/20/marissa-mayer-case-study-in-poor-leadership/?sh=1c8c91c73b46
Lead Change Group. (n.d.). Communicate the Vision: A Case Study. https://leadchangegroup.com/communicate-vision-a-case-study/
Incafrica. (n.d.). Leading with Why: A Case Study on Aaron Skonnard. https://incafrica.com/library/aaron-skonnard-leading-with-why
Leaders.com. (n.d.). Start with Why: A Case Study on Leadership. https://leaders.com/articles/leadership/start-with-why/
Future State COO. (n.d.). Creating a Shared Vision for Success. https://futurestatecoo.com/blog/shared-vision
Risely. (n.d.). Strategic Thinking Examples for Managers.
https://www.risely.me/strategic-thinking-examples-for-managers/#Examples_of_strategic_thinking_skills_of_companies_that_succeeded

Chapter 8

Habitify. (n.d.). Why Goal Setting Is Important for Leaders.
https://www.habitify.me/blog/why-goal-setting-is-important-for-leaders
Insightlopedia. (n.d.). Bring Your Vision to Life with SMART Goals. https://www.insightlopedia.com/articles/bring-your-vision-to-life-with-smart-goals
Vantage Circle. (n.d.). Leadership SMART Goals: A Complete Guide. https://blog.vantagecircle.com/leadership-smart-goals/
Develop Good Habits. (n.d.). SMART Goals: Definition, Importance, and Examples.
https://www.developgoodhabits.com/smart-goals-work/

Notejoy. (n.d.). SMART Goals Examples for Work. https://notejoy.com/resources/smart-goals-examples-for-work

BetterUp. (n.d.). SMART Goals: Definition, Examples, and Tips. https://www.betterup.com/blog/smart-goals

Preply. (n.d.). B2B SMART Goals Examples for Work. https://preply.com/en/blog/b2b-smart-goals-examples-for-work/

Leaders.com. (n.d.). Goal Setting: A Key to Success in Leadership. https://leaders.com/articles/personal-growth/goal-setting/

Flock. (n.d.). How to Set SMART Goals: A Complete Guide. https://blog.flock.com/set-smart-goals

Fellow. (n.d.). The Ultimate Guide to Leadership SMART Goals (With Examples). https://fellow.app/blog/leadership/leadership-smart-goals-guide-examples/

Clockify. (n.d.). SMART Goals: A Complete Guide with Examples. https://clockify.me/blog/productivity/smart-goals/

Forbes Business Council. (2021, December 9). The One Leadership Quality That You Need: Decision-Making. https://www.forbes.com/sites/forbesbusinesscouncil/2021/12/09/the-one-leadership-quality-that-you-need-decision-making/?sh=7338d1c3f598

Indeed. (n.d.). Why Is Decision-Making an Important Leadership Skill? https://www.indeed.com/career-advice/career-development/why-is-decision-making-an-important-leadership-skill

Program on Negotiation at Harvard Law School. (n.d.). Leadership and Decision-Making: Empowering Better Decisions. https://www.pon.harvard.edu/daily/leadership-skills-daily/leadership-and-decision-making-empowering-better-decisions/

Community Tool Box. (n.d.). Making Decisions. https://ctb.ku.edu/en/table-of-contents/leadership/leadership-functions/make-decisions/main

Indeed. (n.d.). Decision-Making Style: What It Is and Why It's Important. https://www.indeed.com/career-advice/career-development/decision-making-style

Alloy Strong. (n.d.). Case Study: Decision Making. https://www.alloystrong.com/blog/case-study-decision-making

Harvard Business Review. (2018, April). The Power of Leaders Who Focus on Solving Problems. https://hbr.org/2018/04/the-power-of-leaders-who-focus-on-solving-problems

Robert Half. (n.d.). Why Are Problem-Solving Skills Essential in Leadership? https://www.roberthalf.jp/en/blog/employers/why-are-problem-solving-skills-essential-leadership

Florida Tech Online. (n.d.). Problem Solving: A Critical Leadership Skill. https://www.floridatechonline.com/blog/business/problem-solving-a-critical-leadership-skill/

Skills You Need. (n.d.). Problem Solving and Decision Making (Solving Problems and Making Decisions). https://www.skillsyouneed.com/ips/problem-solving.html

Read This Twice. (n.d.). Quotes from the book "The Power of Habit" by Charles Duhigg. https://www.readthistwice.com/quotes/book/the-power-of-habit

Chapter 9

Leaders Edge, Inc. (n.d.). Three Ways Leaders Fail at Communication. https://www.leadersedgeinc.com/blog/three-ways-leaders-fail-at-communication

Judson Group. (n.d.). The Role of Communication in Leadership. https://www.judson-group.com/role-communication-leadership/

Fast Company. (2014, September 30). 9 Reasons Leaders Fail to Communicate and What to Do About It. https://www.fastcompany.com/3040332/9-reasons-leaders-fail-to-communicate-and-what-to-do-about-it

Harappa Education. (n.d.). Communication for Leaders: Strategies and Skills. https://harappa.education/harappa-diaries/communication-for-leaders/

Skills You Need. (n.d.). Listening Skills. https://www.skillsyouneed.com/ips/listening-skills.html

LinkedIn. (n.d.). Why Listening Is the Most Important Skill a Leader Can Have. https://www.linkedin.com/pulse/listening-most-important-skill-leader-can-have-brigette-hyacinth/

Medium. (n.d.). Skills of a Good Leader: Active Listening. https://medium.com/age-of-awareness/skills-of-a-good-leader-active-listening-24b226d577c

Leaders.com. (n.d.). Active Listening: A Key Leadership Skill. https://leaders.com/articles/leadership/active-listening/

The Enterprisers Project. (2020, July 29). Why Listening Is a Critical Leadership Skill. https://enterprisersproject.com/article/2020/7/listening

Skills You Need. (n.d.). Active Listening. https://www.skillsyouneed.com/ips/active-listening.html

Skills You Need. (n.d.). Effective Speaking: The Importance of Spoken Communication. https://www.skillsyouneed.com/ips/effective-speaking.html

Forbes. (2012, April 4). 10 Communication Secrets of Great Leaders. https://www.forbes.com/sites/mikemyatt/2012/04/04/10-communication-secrets-of-great-leaders/?sh=b4d894822fe9

Harvard Business School Online. (n.d.). Leadership Communication: Crafting a Compelling Story. https://online.hbs.edu/blog/post/leadership-communication

USC Annenberg School for Communication and Journalism. (n.d.). How Leaders Communicate Effectively: 5 Rules. https://communicationmgmt.usc.edu/blog/how-leaders-communicate-effectively-5-rules/

ModernGov. (n.d.). Examples of Effective Communication in the Workplace. https://blog.moderngov.com/examples-of-effective-communication-in-the-workplace

Skills You Need. (n.d.). Conversational Skills. https://www.skillsyouneed.com/ips/conversational-skills.html

Skills You Need. (n.d.). Verbal Communication: Effective Verbal Communication Skills. https://www.skillsyouneed.com/ips/verbal-communication.html

Skills You Need. (n.d.). Rapport: Building and Maintaining Relationships. https://www.skillsyouneed.com/ips/rapport.html

Lighthouse. (n.d.). How to Build Rapport with Your Team. https://getlighthouse.com/blog/build-rapport/

Lighthouse. (n.d.). How to Build Rapport: 6 Simple Steps. https://getlighthouse.com/blog/how-to-build-rapport/

Medium. (n.d.). This Is How Good Leaders Build Rapport With Their People. https://medium.com/@DrNicoleLipkin/this-is-how-good-leaders-build-rapport-with-their-people-84ab52236e88

Skills You Need. (n.d.). Rapport: Building and Maintaining Relationships. https://www.skillsyouneed.com/ips/rapport.html

Tony Robbins. (n.d.). Building Rapport in Business: The Ultimate Guide. https://www.tonyrobbins.com/business/building-rapport-in-business/

Links International. (n.d.). How the Best Leaders Build Rapport With Their Employees. https://linksinternational.com/blog/how-the-best-leaders-build-rapport-with-their-employees/

Chapter 10

Harvard Business School Online. (n.d.). How to Delegate Effectively. https://online.hbs.edu/blog/post/how-to-delegate-effectively

Virgin. (n.d.). Richard Branson: Why Delegation Is Crucial to Success. https://www.virgin.com/about-virgin/latest/richard-branson-why-delegation-crucial-success

Prialto. (n.d.). Why Delegating Is Important: A Guide for Leaders. https://www.prialto.com/blog/delegating-important

Gina Abudi. (n.d.). Learning to Delegate: A Mini Case Study.
https://www.ginaabudi.com/learning-to-delegate-a-mini-case-study/
Inc. (2006, March 1). DAO Leadership: The Power of Delegation.
https://www.inc.com/resources/leadership/articles/20060301/dao.html
Eagle's Flight. (n.d.). The Importance of Delegation for Leadership. https://www.eaglesflight.com/resource/the-importance-of-delegation-for-leadership/
Harvard Business Review. (2017, October). To Be a Great Leader, You Have to Learn How to Delegate Well.
https://hbr.org/2017/10/to-be-a-great-leader-you-have-to-learn-how-to-delegate-well
Skills You Need. (n.d.). Delegation Skills.
https://www.skillsyouneed.com/lead/delegation.html
The Balance Careers. (n.d.). Improve Your Delegation Skills With These Tips.
https://www.thebalancecareers.com/delegation-skills-2059688
SHRM. (n.d.). How to Delegate Effectively: Tips for Leadership Success.
https://www.shrm.org/resourcesandtools/hr-topics/organizational-and-employee-development/pages/delegateeffectively.aspx
Leaders.com. (n.d.). Personal Growth: The Ultimate Guide to Goal Setting. https://leaders.com/articles/personal-growth/goal-setting/

Chapter 11

Zander, B. (2023). The Art of Possibility. Penguin Books. Harlow, England. ISBN 978-0142001103.
Development Academy. (n.d.). The Dangers of Micromanagement: How to Avoid Them.

https://development-academy.co.uk/news-tips/micromanagement/

Fast Company. (2020, August 12). Your Urge to Micromanage is Actually the Result of Bad Communication. https://www.fastcompany.com/90599143/your-urge-to-micromanagement-is-actually-the-result-of-bad-communication

The Uncommon League. (2018, December 9). Understanding Micromanagement: How a Leader's Insecurity Can Make Their Staff Miserable. https://theuncommonleague.com/blog/2018129/understanding-micromanagement-how-a-leaders-insecurity-can-make-their-staff-miserable

Kilday, K. (n.d.). The Pitfalls of Micromanagement. https://kenkilday.com/the-pitfalls-of-micromanagement/

PATimes. (n.d.). Damaging Effects of Micromanagement. https://patimes.org/damaging-effects-micromanagement/

Harvard Business Review. (2015, August 25). How to Stop Micromanaging Your Team. https://hbr.org/2015/08/how-to-stop-micromanaging-your-team

Harvard Business Review. (2021, January 5). How to Help Without Micromanaging. https://hbr.org/2021/01/how-to-help-without-micromanaging

Chron Small Business. (n.d.). Strategies for Avoiding the Micromanagement Trap. https://smallbusiness.chron.com/strategies-avoiding-micromanagement-trap-52904.html

Chapter 12

BetterUp. (n.d.). Autonomy in the Workplace: How to Empower Your Team. https://www.betterup.com/blog/autonomy-in-the-workplace

DecisionWise. (n.d.). Autonomy: Empowering the Individual to Do Their Best Work. https://decision-wise.com/resources/articles/autonomy-empowering-the-individual-to-do-their-best-work/

Matchr. (n.d.). The Power of Employee Autonomy: Why It's Essential and How to Encourage It. https://matchr.com/blog/employee-autonomy/

Harvard Business Review. (2016, October 17). Do You Understand What Accountability Really Means? https://hbr.org/2016/10/do-you-understand-what-accountability-really-means

Hypercontext. (n.d.). Create a Culture of Accountability in the Workplace. https://hypercontext.com/blog/management-skills/create-culture-accountability-workplace

BetterWorks. (n.d.). Accountability in Leadership: How to Develop It in Your Team. https://www.betterworks.com/magazine/accountability-in-leadership/

PepTalk. (n.d.). Leadership Accountability: How to Lead by Example. https://www.peptalk.com/post/leadership-accountability

Harvard Business Review. (2020, November 20). How to Actually Encourage Employee Accountability. https://hbr.org/2020/11/how-to-actually-encourage-employee-accountability

Flock. (n.d.). The Benefits of Team Collaboration at Work. https://blog.flock.com/benefits-team-collaboration-work

Jostle. (n.d.). Why Collaboration Is Important: The Benefits of Collaboration in the Workplace. https://blog.jostle.me/blog/why-collaboration-is-important

Kissflow. (n.d.). The Importance of Collaboration in the Workplace. https://kissflow.com/digital-workplace/collaboration/importance-of-collaboration-in-the-workplace/

HubSpot. (n.d.). Team Collaboration: What It Is and Why It's Important. https://blog.hubspot.com/service/team-collaboration

Ohio State University. (n.d.). Leadership Guide to Conflict and Conflict Management. https://ohiostate.pressbooks.pub/publhlmp6615/chapter/leadership-guide-to-conflict-and-conflict-management/

Mattice, Z. (n.d.). Resolving Conflict: A Case Study. https://www.linkedin.com/pulse/resolving-conflict-case-study-mattice-zundel-ma-sphr-shrm-scp/

North Central College. (2022, September 13). Why Conflict Resolution is Important. https://www.northcentralcollege.edu/news/2022/09/13/why-conflict-resolution-important

Vantage Circle. (n.d.). Conflict Resolution in the Workplace: A Complete Guide. https://blog.vantagecircle.com/conflict-resolution-in-the-workplace/

Leaders.com. (n.d.). Conflict Resolution Skills Every Leader Needs. https://leaders.com/articles/leadership/conflict-resolution-skills/

Harvard Business Review. (2017, July 11). How to Handle a Disagreement on Your Team. https://hbr.org/2017/07/how-to-handle-a-disagreement-on-your-team

St. Catherine University. (n.d.). Conflict Resolution Strategies. https://www.stkate.edu/academics/women-in-leadership-degrees/conflict-resolution-strategies

Michael Page. (n.d.). Why Dealing with Conflict Has Positive Outcomes. https://www.michaelpage.com.au/advice/management-advice/staff-development/why-dealing-conflict-has-positive-outcomes

CameloHQ. (n.d.). 5 Types of Workplace Conflicts and How to Deal With Them. https://blog.camelohq.com/5-types-of-workplace-conflicts/

Program on Negotiation at Harvard Law School. (n.d.). Types of Conflict. https://www.pon.harvard.edu/daily/conflict-resolution/types-conflict/

LiveAbout. (n.d.). How to Lead the Team: How to Become the Person Others Follow. https://www.liveabout.com/lead-the-team-how-to-become-the-person-others-follow-1918610

Harvard Business Review. (2020, May 5). Good Leadership is About Communicating "Why". https://hbr.org/2020/05/good-leadership-is-about-communicating-why

RDP Associates. (n.d.). 5 Ways to Vastly Improve Strategic Visioning in Leadership. https://www.rdpusa.com/5-ways-vastly-improve-strategic-visioning-leadership/

Community Tool Box. (n.d.). Developing and Communicating a Vision. https://ctb.ku.edu/en/table-of-contents/leadership/leadership-functions/develop-and-communicate-vision/main

Skills You Need. (n.d.). Developing a Compelling Vision. https://www.skillsyouneed.com/lead/compelling-vision.html

Skills You Need. (n.d.). Communicating the Vision. https://www.skillsyouneed.com/lead/communicating-vision.html

Printed in Great Britain
by Amazon

45363436R00165